COPING SKILLS FOR TEENS WITH AUTISM

EFFECTIVE TIPS AND HELPFUL STRATEGIES FOR TEENS ON THE AUTISM SPECTRUM TO BUILD AND NAVIGATE SOCIAL SKILLS AT HOME, SCHOOL AND IN THE COMMUNITY

R ROBINSON

Copyright © 2023 R. Robinson. All rights reserved.

The content within this book may not be reproduced, duplicated, or transmitted without direct written permission from the author or the publisher.

Under no circumstances will any blame or legal responsibility be held against the publisher, or author, for any damages, reparation, or monetary loss due to the information contained within this book, either directly or indirectly.

Legal Notice:

This book is copyright protected. It is only for personal use. You cannot amend, distribute, sell, use, quote, or paraphrase any part of the content within this book, without the consent of the author or publisher.

Disclaimer Notice:

Please note the information contained within this document is for educational and entertainment purposes only. All effort has been expended to present accurate, up-to-date, reliable, and complete information. No warranties of any kind are declared or implied. Readers acknowledge that the author is not engaged in the rendering of legal, financial, medical, or professional advice. The content within this book has been derived from various sources. Please consult a licensed professional before attempting any techniques outlined in this book.

By reading this document, the reader agrees that under no circumstances is the author responsible for any losses, direct or indirect, that are incurred as a result of the use of the information contained within this document, including, but not limited to, errors, omissions, or inaccuracies.

CONTENTS

Introduction   7

1. WHAT IS AUTISM SPECTRUM SYNDROME?   13
   Teens' Autism Symptoms and Signs   15
   Symptoms of Autism in Teens   16
   Teenage Autistic Behavior Indicators.   19
   Sensory Sensitivities   20
   Causes of Autism Spectrum Syndrome   23
   Complications.   26
   Types of Autism   31

2. HOW TO KNOW AN AUTISTIC TEEN IS HAVING A HARD TIME COPING   35
   Signs that a teen with autism is struggling to cope   36
   Emotions   37
   Autistic Burnout   40
   How can Autistic Teens Deal with Burnout?   42
   Having Challenges in Specific Social Circumstances.   43
   How to Aid Teens with Autism in Recognizing Emotions   46
   Anxiety   49
   Having Communication problems   50

3. WHAT ARE TRIGGERS?   53
   Guidelines for Identifying Autism Meltdown Triggers   53
   Sensory overload   69

4. WHY BUILD COPING SKILLS? 73
   Coping Skills for Managing Emotions 76
   Why Teens with Autism Find Emotions Difficult 76
   Anger Management 78
   Improving Communication with Coping Skills 79
   Taking Care of Sensory Overload 80
   Sensory overload signs and symptoms. 81
   What triggers sensory overload? 81

5. TYPES OF COPING SKILLS 85
   1. Focused Problem-Solving Skills 85
   2. Emotional Coping Skills 86
   Yoga for Autism. 87
   Deep Breathing Exercise 89
   Relaxation Exercise 90
   Meditation 91
   Relaxation through Body Scan Visualization. 96
   Making Meaning 97
   Reframing 97
   Journaling 104

6. COPING STRATEGIES FOR AUTISTIC TEENS 111
   Deep Breathing Exercise 112
   Breathe Focus 115
   Equal Breathing Time. 116
   Progressive Relaxation of the Muscles. 117
   Mindfulness 118
   Exercise 121
   Visualization 127
   Music 127
   Taking a Leisure Walk. 128
   Do something enjoyable and relaxing. 128

Activities for Coping with Autism in
Teens | 129
15 Coping Activities for Teens with
Autism | 139

7. HOW TO COPE WITH AUTISM WHILE
AT SCHOOL | 149
Signs of classroom anxiety | 151
Strategies for Familiarizing Oneself and
Practicing for School Anxiety | 153
Helping Your Teen to Cope with
AUTISM in the Classroom | 156
Strategies For Handling Classroom
Behavior Issues Associated With Autism. | 162

8. COPING WITH AUTISM IN SOCIAL
ENVIRONMENT | 169
Social Interaction Skills for Teens with
Autism | 169
Developing play skills | 174
Social Skills Development for Teens with
Autism | 179
How to Train Autistic Teenagers to Act
Correctly in Social Settings. | 183

9. HOW TO DETERMINE IF THE COPING
SKILLS ARE HELPING | 193
Reduction in Anxiety | 194
Reduction of tantrums and Meltdowns | 195
Reduced sensory overload | 196
Increased Interaction with Others | 197
Improve communication skills | 200

10. EXPLORE AUTISM SPECTRUM
DISORDER THERAPY | 203
The Significance of Offering Therapy | 204
The Significance of giving therapy to
Autistic Teens | 208
Therapies for autism. | 209

Treatments for the conditions that
frequently go along with autism. 223
Maximizing the benefits of therapy. 225

Conclusion 233
Bibliography 235

INTRODUCTION

Coping strategies are ways we control our thoughts, emotions, and behaviors to endure, reduce, and handle difficult life circumstances.

Coping skills for autism are defined as "means that can assist autistic teens in returning to or maintaining a regulated state, which can be viewed as a wide range of various kinds of strategies ranging from sensory-based coping skills, such as playdoh to cognitive approach such as puzzles for teens with autism.

As a parent, Coping skills are crucial in your arsenal when unanticipated, unclear, or tense situations occur and your teen requires additional support to settle down.

But how can you determine what suits your teen best and adopt a plan for their emotions?

- **Recognizing Their Emotions**

Your autistic teen needs to be able to recognize and name emotions before introducing coping skills.

It can be challenging for autistic teens to identify, name, and comprehend complicated emotions or sensations of several emotions at once, so teaching your teen the various emotional categories is one method to help them acquire an understanding of emotions.

Using regular encounters is a quick and effective way to help your autistic teen understand emotions and develop their capacity to communicate and cope with them.

Here are a few concepts:

- **Identify Emotions in your Surroundings**

You can draw attention to emotions when you and your teen are reading a book, viewing a video, or going to a friend's house.

For instance, you might say, "Look like Dad is laughing. He is pleased!"

- **Be receptive**

React to your child's feelings by saying, "You're smiling, so you must be happy."

You could also try exaggerating your feelings, such as saying, "I'm SO excited!" I want a high five.

- **Use tools to make the process more visible.**

Use mood cards with images of actual or animated features to demonstrate how certain feelings correspond with particular facial expressions.

Play card games concerning facial expressions and challenge your autistic teen to match the emotions to the word or phrase that best describes them.

Use social stories to describe social circumstances to your teen by incorporating both their feelings and the feelings of others into a drawn narrative or cartoon strip.

EDUCATING AUTISTIC TEENS TO CONTROL THEIR EMOTIONS

Your autistic teen is prepared to take the next stage, learning to control his feelings and develop coping skills, now that he can recognize and categorize the various emotions.

Strong emotional control skills enable autistic teens to:

- Recognize when they start to become upset
- Know when they are about to experience a meltdown and how to apply the necessary coping skills.
- Think about the effects of their response.
- Identify potential triggers and how to regulate it
- Cope in a social environment

Coping skills are a vital tool needed by autistic teens in regulating their emotions, understanding and coping with the social environment, schoolwork, making and keeping friends, adjusting to the work environment, and thriving and succeeding in society.

As a parent, you are vital in teaching your autistic teen the much-needed coping skills to help them thrive and live independently as adults.

Below are some vital steps to help you get started.

Let's get straight to teaching your autistic teen how to manage their autism.

1. Teach Coping Strategies

Choose coping strategies for your teen to use when experiencing these emotions, and have your child exercise them. You can do this by posing scenarios to your teen and having role-plays about how to apply the solutions you've come up with together.

If your autistic teen learns better visually, you can also use a grid. For example, having icons or images to represent that strategy.

2. Develop an Emotional Level Chart

Create a graphical tool with your teen that illustrates the various emotional levels they might experience, and let them name each level. For instance, if you're working on the emotion "Happiness," you can sketch a smiley face with your teen and let them write the adjectives "very happy," "feeling good," etc. on it.

Give them an empty sheet "I feel this way when..." section to complete.

3. Show your teen how to categorize circumstances.

There are two methods to accomplish this.

One is to discuss with your different teen situations that would cause particular feelings and then jot them down. You could, for instance, ask the question:

- "When are you happy?"
- "What brings you joy?"

Two, you can go the other route and ask your teen how they would feel in various situations while presenting them such. Ask them, for instance, how they would feel if they weren't permitted to go to the playground.

4. Go over the proper responses to various situations.

Go through the list with your child and discuss which response is suitable for each circumstance once you have determined which situations your child thinks are linked to each emotion.

For instance, if your kid expresses "Very Angry" about being unable to go to the playground, you can first acknowledge their emotions by saying, "I can see why you would be outraged." Then you can explain why you should feel unhappy rather than angry.

Your child will learn that different emotional intensity levels exist, and some circumstances can be less intense.

With this final point, I think you are prepared to assist your autistic teen in finding the coping skills that are most effective for them but keep in mind that this process is continuous one.

1

WHAT IS AUTISM SPECTRUM SYNDROME?

The term autism spectrum syndrome refers to a wide variety of neurological disorders identifiable by particular mannerisms, modes of speech, and social interaction patterns.

Autism is referred to as a "spectrum disorder" because, when contrasted to what is neurotypical, or essentially what many would refer to as the "social norm," the external symptoms of autism can vary on a continuum from "mild" (not very obvious) to "severe" (very obvious).

Doctors can determine autism spectrum syndrome by pointing out a few crucial symptoms, according to the Diagnostic and Statistical Manual of Mental Disorders, Fifth Edition (DSM-5).

The symptoms of autism, however, differ significantly from person to person, and as you mature, the symptoms can also change:

The ASD symptoms you display as a child may differ from those you experience as a teen.

Let's discuss the typical symptoms of ASD in teens, what to do if your teen has the disorder, and what to do if you're worried that autism will interfere with your or your teen's daily life.

When do these symptoms usually start to show up?

The symptoms of ASD can vary as people age. Autism is frequently impossible to identify unless its symptoms appear when your child is young so that a behavior trend can be formed.

And, there is no set period during which your adolescent will exhibit these symptoms of autism. However, as with many teenagers, when they reach adolescence, typically between the ages of 11 and 13, you might notice behavioral and hormonal changes.

When a child enters middle and high school, during which social interactions frequently take on a more significant role in a teen's life, autistic symptoms might also start to become more apparent.

TEENS' AUTISM SYMPTOMS AND SIGNS

We've detailed the signs that an autistic child may experience as they enter adolescence if you're concerned that your teen may be autistic or if you have an autistic teen and want to know what to anticipate when they're young.

Additionally, you'll discover what to do if you know a teen has autism and management techniques for specific habits.

Why do some teens receive a diagnosis years later?

A late diagnosis is frequently made if a young individual is "high functioning" or intellectually capable.

Additionally, girls are more proficient than boys at mimicking neuro-typical behaviors, such as vocal and nonverbal communication, to hide their autism, so girls experience this more often than boys.

Because of some uncertainty, it can be challenging to determine whether a child has autism or since other conditions have manifested as their paramount need, such as another medical condition like ADHD.

Children typically adapt well to primary school settings but find the increased demands of secondary school very distressing, making their autistic condition more apparent.

SYMPTOMS OF AUTISM IN TEENS

If a parent, instructor, or career suspects a teen may have autism, there are some symptoms they should watch out for:

1. Problems with the sensory perception

- Issues of emotional stimulation, such as finding school commotion too much.
- Not being able to handle lines or crowds.
- Not touchable and sensitive.
- Need help organizing and arranging their day at school, their job, or their luggage.

2. Emotional challenges

- Having a low self-esteem
- Having an inability or unwillingness to name or articulate their feelings.
- Having levels of worry that seem out of proportion to the precipitating circumstance.
- Melancholy or a low disposition.
- A wish to cut oneself off from the world.

Teenagers with autism vary from other kids in how they use vocal and unconscious speech for social reasons.

Verbal Communication

Teenagers with autism may:

- Find it difficult to switch off during talks; they might prefer to speak all the time or struggle to provide honest responses to a personal fascination
- Speak a lot about their areas of expertise, but find it challenging to discuss various subjects or things they don't find particularly fascinating.
- Take everything seriously; they might find the phrase "Pull your socks up!" confusing. And genuinely put their hosiery on.
- Have different accents or methods of speaking from other kids, such as speaking very clearly or with an accent or not varying the loudness or tone of their voices.
- Use polite words and excellent vocabulary.
- Find more than 1-2 stages challenging to follow.

Nonverbal Communication

Teenagers with autism may:

- Have trouble interpreting visual signals, such as body language or speech tone, to infer how another person is feeling. For instance, they might not be able to recognize when someone is making fun of them or being sarcastic.
- Do not use much eye contact or less eye contact than other individuals.
- They have less feeling on their faces than other kids or are unable to interpret other people's reactions to their features, such as being unable to tell when someone is tired.
- Use only a few motions to communicate.

4. Establishing Connections and Friendships.

Teenagers with autism may:

- They prefer to spend their free time alone rather than with friends.
- If their standards aren't observed, they become angry and want others to play by their rules.
- Need help comprehending the conventions of companionship in society.

- Have few or no friends and find it challenging to make new ones.
- Prefer to engage with smaller kids or adults and struggle to relate to most kids their age.
- Need help changing their conduct in various social settings.
- Be more at ease in a small personal area than others.

TEENAGE AUTISTIC BEHAVIOR INDICATORS.

Repetitive habits and passions.

Teenagers with autism may:

- Possess unique or specific hobbies. For instance, they may gather sticks or remember football stats but need to be more genuinely engaged in the sport.
- Have actions that appear obsessive, such as shutting all the doorways in the home or arranging items.
- Be especially sentimental about certain things; for instance, they might gather trinkets or amass objects like chip packages or shoelaces.
- Be sensitive to change and enjoy rituals; for instance, they may need to be informed in advance when a difference to their regular

schedule is coming up, or they may have a daily routine for getting ready.
- They may mimic motions or move their limbs in unusual ways, such as flapping their hands or rocking back and forth.
- Take pleasure in producing repeated sounds, such as squeals, vocal clearings, or groans.

SENSORY SENSITIVITIES

Teenagers with autism may:

- Be mindful of the olfactory surroundings; they may be more easily offended by loud sounds than other people, dislike clothing marks, or only consume foods of a particular texture or hue.
- They might enjoy intense pressure, look for moving items like laundry machines, or place their fingertips in front of their eyes to watch a light flash as a visual stimulus.
- Compared to other teens, they react to discomfort less.

Teens with autism frequently also struggle with other problems. These could consist of the following:

Sleeping problems

For instance, they might have trouble sleeping, wake up frequently, or have irregular sleeping habits.

Anxiety

Anxiety may lead to meltdowns or overwhelming feelings. For instance, they might experience anxiety when visiting new locations or participating in large-group social settings.

Depression

Teens with autism who know their differences are frequently conscious of how others perceive them. They might experience alienation and face bullying from others due to their peculiarities.

It may result in depressed moods, which puberty's increasing hormone levels may exacerbate.

Aggressive Attitude

Teenagers with autism frequently experience sensory hypersensitivity, which can cause impulsive and occasionally violent behavior. They might find it challenging to comprehend what is happening around them, and they may become increasingly frustrated as a result, which they cannot regulate immediately.

Eating Problems

Teenagers with autism may create these as a means of managing their surroundings. For instance, teenagers may struggle to transition to secondary education and turn to food disorders as a coping mechanism for nervousness.

Executive Dysfunction Issues

The brain processes require planning, organizing ideas and actions, setting priorities, and effectively controlling time.

Teenagers with autism may struggle to handle certain parts of secondary education, like complicated schedules, as a result of these challenges.

School Rejection or Avoidance

Teenagers with autism may experience stress or confusion at school. Additionally, they might be at risk for abuse at school.

Pressure to cope with daily activities at school can make autistic teens want to reject or try to avoid school as much as possible.

If your teen is aware of their autism, they can better understand themselves, take pride in who they are, and make friends with people who think, engage, and learn similarly.

CAUSES OF AUTISM SPECTRUM SYNDROME

The origin of autism spectrum syndrome is unknown. There are presumably numerous reasons, given the disorder's intricacy and the reality that symptoms and intensity differ.

Environment and heredity are both important.

Genetics.

Autism spectrum syndrome appears to be caused by several distinct genes. For some kids, a hereditary condition like Rett syndrome or Fragile X syndrome may be linked to autistic spectrum disorder.

Other children may be more susceptible to autistic spectrum disorder due to hereditary alterations (mutations).

Other traits may influence how the brain develops, how brain cells interact, or even how severe a condition is. While some DNA changes appear to be transmitted, others happen independently.

External Variables.

Scientists are examining whether environmental toxins, medicines, reproductive problems, and viral illnesses can cause autism spectrum syndrome.

No connection exists between autistic spectrum symptoms and immunizations, and whether there is a connection between autistic spectrum disorder and infant immunizations is one of the biggest questions in the field.

Despite considerable research, no credible study has established a connection between immunization and autistic spectrum syndrome.

The initial study that started the discussion years ago has been withdrawn because of its flawed design and dubious research techniques.

Neglecting childhood immunizations puts your kid and others at risk of contracting and sharing dangerous illnesses like measles, mumps, and whooping cough.

Risk Factors

The percentage of teens receiving an autistic spectrum disorder diagnosis is growing.

It's unclear whether this is the result of improved identification and reporting, a substantial rise in the number of instances, or a combination of the two, and teens of all ethnicities and countries are affected by autism spectrum disorder. Still, certain variables make a teen more likely to develop it.

These may consist of the following:

- **Sex of your kid.**

The risk of developing autistic spectrum syndrome is roughly four times higher in males than females.

- **Family background.**

Families with one kid diagnosed with autistic spectrum syndrome are likelier to have another child with the condition.

Additionally, it's not unusual for parents or other family members of a kid with an autistic spectrum syndrome to exhibit some of the disorder's hallmark behaviors or to experience minor difficulties with their social or speech abilities.

- **Other Health Conditions**

Children who have certain medical problems are more likely than average to develop autism spectrum disorder or signs that are similar to autism.

Examples include Rett syndrome, a genetic disorder almost exclusively affecting girls that slow head growth, intellectual disability, and the loss of purposeful hand use; fragile X syndrome, a hereditary condition that causes cognitive problems; tuberous sclerosis, a medical condition in which typical tumors develop in the brain.

- **Extremely Premature Infants.**

Babies delivered before 26 weeks of pregnancy may more likely develop autistic spectrum syndrome.

- **Age of parents.**

More study is required to determine whether there is a relationship between the autistic spectrum condition and children delivered to elderly parents.

COMPLICATIONS.

Social contact, dialogue, and conduct issues can result in the following:

- Problems with learning successfully and at school.

- Issues with employment.
- An inability to support oneself.
- Isolated from society.
- Stress at home or school.
- Bullying and being a victim.

What must you do if you suspect your teen has autism?

Autism cannot be cured. Your teen's demeanor and sense of self are reflected in it, and If your teen is concerned about not fitting in, help them learn to embrace and respect themselves.

Consult an autism-focused doctor, psychologist, or therapist first. They will be able to guide you through the process of diagnosing autism, which includes:

- Checking off typical growth stages as you observe your teen's progress.
- Performing a thorough behavioral assessment
- Identify the tools to help your teen surmount obstacles to neurotypical standards and self-sufficiency.

How can you help a teen with autism?

Every autistic person will experience mixed results, just as every person has distinct autism symptoms. The first thing to realize is that your teen is not handicapped or lacking in anything.

Nevertheless, based on how serious or moderate the autism has been deemed to be, they might need access to tools that can assist them in overcoming difficulties in adjusting to neurotypical standards and daily living.

Here's how to help your autistic teen love and embrace themselves while making them feel accepted and loved by you and the people around them.

1. Find out more about autism.

There seem to be new tools for learning and coping with autism daily. Speak with medical professionals, academics, or speech therapists who specialize in autism to learn:

- More information on how autism functions,
- How a neurodivergent brain functions
- How to speak up for your autistic teen when other people don't embrace or comprehend who they are?

2. Discover every aspect of your autistic teen.

Typically, parents act this way, and it drives most teens nuts.

- Ask your teen about the emotions and feelings they are experiencing if you're unsure what to do.
- Keep the lines of communication open with your teen.
- Request their views in writing or ask them to share them with you.

It's essential to watch your teen's behavior and keep track of any potential triggers if they aren't verbally or in writing with you to express their thoughts or feelings.

- Find out what works and what doesn't to reduce habits that might be distracting or make it harder for them to make the most of the tools they can access.

Try to reduce those stressors or give your adolescent coping skills if you think their behavior is upsetting or impeding their ability to thrive in ways they've voiced interest.

Here are a few ideas.

Do bright lights cause them distress? Keep your home's light low.

Do loud sounds distract them or overwhelm their senses? Purchase some earbuds or noise-canceling headphones.

Your adolescent may be experiencing strong feelings. Be patient and give them some room. Avoid yelling, making them feel guilty, or retaliating violently or with cruel words.

Embrace them as they are.

There is nothing amiss with your teen despite what many parents of autistic teenagers hear from others and groups.

They don't require repair. Make them feel loved and cherished. Invite them to all of your family's gatherings. Please participate in the pursuits they enjoy.

Respect their limits by granting them solitude when they request it or by allowing them to have their peers and interests.

Be dependable and encouraging.

Your teen's autism represents the following traits:

Personality

Cognition

Emotion

Selfhood

Being there for your teen is essential as they deal with the expectation to fit in with neurotypical norms in addition to the typical teenage challenges.

Maintaining a supportive atmosphere can considerably impact the course of their lives long after they reach adulthood.

Support can also be provided by teaching your adolescent specific life skills or habits they might find challenging.

TYPES OF AUTISM

You can spot early symptoms in your kid by being aware of the various types of autism.

The first step in assisting a child in living a fulfilling and happy life is determining what autism they have, as an increasing number of kids are getting an autism designation.

There are various forms of autism, including:

1. *Grade 1 ASD*

Some people refer to this as "high-functioning" autism. Persons with Level 1 ASD frequently battle with social signals and show a strong passion for just one or two topics.

A speech impediment does not frequently accompany this form of autism, and in some instances, kids may display an advanced lexicon for their age.

2. Rett Syndrome

In recent years, Rett's Syndrome was removed from the autistic levels. However, it mainly impacts females and first shows up around the age of six months.

Social contact difficulties and diminished hand use (such as trouble with coarse and fine motor skills or repeated hand and arm flailing) are signs of Rett's syndrome, also present in autistic spectrum disorders.

3. Childhood Disintegration Disorder (CDD)

You may have heard tales of kids growing normally and meeting all their developmental milestones until they hit a block and started to decline around the age of two.

Due to the uncertainty and dread it frequently causes, this variety of autism can seem particularly devastating to parents.

Children who had previously appeared to be maturing normally and were sociably engaging chatted made eye contact, abruptly stopped being who they were, and closed down.

According to medical professionals, seizure-causing illnesses and this particular form of autism are related.

4. Kenner Syndrome

When people picture autistic individuals, they typically picture those with Kanner's Syndrome.

The signs of this form of autism, also called Classic Autistic Disorder, include difficulties speaking with or comprehending others, hardly any eye contact, and intolerance to stimulation such as touch, smell, light, taste, or noise.

Children with Kanner's Syndrome exhibit a strong need for order and frequently show no interest in their surroundings. These young people focus inward and don't want to engage with others.

5. Pervasive Development Disorder- Not Otherwise Specified (PDD-NOS).

Compared to other forms of autism, this one is typically less serious. People with this form of autism may have suffered setbacks in developmental landmarks like speaking or walking, and they frequently fall behind other kids who are on track to reach these milestones.

People with PDD-NOS can better control the signs of this lesser type of autism than those with more severe varieties.

In the next chapter, I will discuss how to know an autistic teen is having a hard time coping. See you there.

2

HOW TO KNOW AN AUTISTIC TEEN IS HAVING A HARD TIME COPING

Teens with autism commonly experience ups and downs, and the hormonal changes during adolescence cause these ups and downs.

And having autism can make adolescence more difficult. Teens with autism spectrum syndrome may experience emotional swings that are more intense and common than those experienced by typically growing teens.

Public or private emotional meltdowns or tantrums may come from this, and these tantrums and meltdowns can leave you as a parent feeling helpless and powerless.

SIGNS THAT A TEEN WITH AUTISM IS STRUGGLING TO COPE

You may experience: Mood fluctuations, impatience, rage, and tearfulness, on top of more overt signs like these:

- Significant variations in sleep patterns, weight, food behaviors, or other regular routines
- Losing interest in their customary passions or giving up activities they adore
- Withdrawal from peers, family, and society more than normal
- Rescheduling appointments with their closest pals and giving little to no notice
- Academic challenges that seem new or more complicated, such as passing exams in their favored topic or declining to complete assignments that used to seem simple
- Continuous concerns or ideas that won't go away
- Refusing to express their concerns, despite your best efforts to create a secure environment for a candid conversation about complex subjects.
- Obsession with a specific objective, potentially with the conviction that failure to accomplish it will change everything about their existence.

- Use of drugs or other harmful substances
- Cuts, burns, bruises, and other self-harm indications that your adolescent attempts to conceal or is unable to convincingly explain
- Sexual behavior or desire that appears to be emerging or intensifying
- If physical aggression is not their usual reaction, acting out physically.
- Intense angst over slight differences in routine (trembling, crying, yelling, fleeing from home).
- Persistently seeking confirmation about imagined risks.
- Loss of pleasure in previously gratifying pursuits.
- Panic or avoidance of social settings.
- Obsession with pathogens, pollution, or another imagined danger.
- Practicing Ritualistic actions repeatedly, such as continuous cleansing of hands.

EMOTIONS

Teens without autism are more likely to have emotional breakdowns when overloaded or overstimulated than when attempting to establish independence. Most adolescents experience mood fluctuations due to hormone changes and are more likely to initiate conflicts over obtaining freedom.

Teens with autism may be more susceptible to intense emotions but struggle to express their feelings. They might be more prone to perceive feelings on a visceral level before examining their emotions, making them more prone to withdraw before comprehending why they might be feeling stressed.

When autistic teens experience emotional meltdowns, their bodies go into fight or flight mode because they are unable to control the physical stimuli from their surroundings, which are perceived as dangers by their bodies.

Possible indicators of an autistic meltdown:

- Hysterical sobbing
- Stimming
- Bolting
- Screaming
- Aggression
- Overwhelming anger, worry, or feelings of powerlessness
- Problems with assimilation or excessive sensory stimuli.
- Not using speech abilities to communicate requirements or feelings.

Meltdown ends when they exhaust themselves or when effective coping strategies help to calm them down.

Why do meltdowns occur?

Sudden emotional eruptions are common, which don't always result from confrontation. The physical over-stimulation of a setting, especially in public or strange locations, is frequently linked to meltdowns.

Teens with autism who experience anxiety have a dread of changes in habit, new surroundings, unfamiliar people, and changes. However, it is often feasible to identify potential anxious triggers; teens with autism profit from highly organized rituals and consistency to help them handle out-of-control emotions.

Meltdowns typically arise from the following:

- When a teenager with ASD has trouble recognizing the emotions they're experiencing
- When they are unable to control their feelings.
- When they are unable to communicate their feelings in any other way.

A loop of self-defeating ideas that could lead to a breakdown may be exacerbated by the feeling of being unable to communicate their feelings in a different way or comprehend them better.

AUTISTIC BURNOUT

Autistic burnout is a sign that a teen with autism is struggling to cope.

What is Autistic Burnout?

The extreme physical, mental, or emotional exhaustion that some teenagers with autism experience are "autistic burnout," which can often be accompanied by a loss of skills.

Many autistic people claim that the combined impact of navigating a world made for people without autism is the leading cause of their condition.

Autistic teens with strong cognitive and social interaction skills who work or attend school with people without autism may be more susceptible to burnout.

I will discuss the latest developments picture of this phenomenon, how burnout in autistic teens might be treated, and how to avoid it altogether.

What is the nature of the autistic burnout experience?

Autistic burnout is one of many characteristics of autism that varies significantly from person to person. Burnout can feel like overwhelming physical exhaustion to some autistic people. They might find it harder than usual to control their feelings and be more prone to angry or sad outbursts.

Burnout can cause severe anxiety, depression, or suicidal thoughts and actions. It might involve increased autism-related characteristics like repetitive actions, heightened sensory sensitivity, or resistance to change.

Loss of skills due to burnout is occasionally possible:

A teenager with autism who typically has good verbal skills might suddenly be unable to express themselves.

How did the idea of burnout come about?

Autistic burnout has not been formally investigated in many studies. Burnout is a phenomenon that autism researchers have only recently become aware of, and through conversations with autistic people in person or online, they have directly learned about it.

The idea reflects the expanding self-advocacy movement within the autism community, prompting researchers to pay closer attention to autistic teens and their inner experiences.

It's not entirely new, though: Some researchers have noted that when overcome by the demands of a challenging environment, teens with autism may have meltdowns or lose skills.

Why does burnout occur?

Burnout is frequently a result of camouflaging, also known as masking, a technique used by autistic people to mimic neurotypical behavior. This technique involves using scripts for small talk, imposing eye contact, and suppressing repetitive behaviors.

These techniques can benefit autistic people in their careers and relationships but are incredibly labor-intensive.

It may also be brought on by sensory overloads, such as that brought on by a noisy bus ride, executive function demands, like those who must manage too many tasks at once, or stress brought on by change.

HOW CAN AUTISTIC TEENS DEAL WITH BURNOUT?

How to handle autistic burnout depends on the individual, but the first step for autistic teens is to get out of the circumstance that caused the burnout.

It could be as easy as returning home to a quiet and relaxing room after a day of erratic interactions with others at school.

Some people might take longer to recover from burnout, and according to some autistic people, burnout can be so severe that its effects can last for years. Burnout may happen more frequently as people age and be harder to recover from.

Is burnout something that can be avoided?

Self-awareness is a necessary preventative measure for burnout. Autistic teens can gradually learn which circumstances are most likely to lead to burnout.

Additionally, they can keep an eye out for these warning signs of impending burnout:

In this state, some autistic people report feeling detached from their bodies or having tunnel vision.

With this knowledge, they can create preventative strategies, such as leaving a social gathering early or scheduling a recovery day after a trip before returning to school.

Additionally, they can request modifications that make it simpler for them to avoid burnout, like preboarding a plane or working part-time from home.

HAVING CHALLENGES IN SPECIFIC SOCIAL CIRCUMSTANCES.

For teens with autism, social circumstances can cause worry and tension. Certain circumstances, such as those in which they are uncertain or with somebody they may not feel secure around, can be challenging and upsetting.

Experiencing excessive physical stimulation.

Teens with autism spectrum disorder have sensitive sensory systems, so environments with loud music, sudden unexpected noises, bright colors, bright lights, and other potentially overstimulating or sudden, surprising things can set off an autistic person's triggers.

Feeling Misunderstood

Humans have a natural desire to fit in and be understood by others, but some actions linked to autistic spectrum disorder may be complex for others to comprehend.

An autistic teen may become defensive, withdrawn, and resentful of someone who didn't demonstrate comprehension.

Unexpected adjustments to habit and surroundings.

For some autistic individuals, routine and understanding what to anticipate is beneficial. A provoked response may result from a shift in a teen with autism's classroom or a disturbance in their school routine.

Even activities and encounters not related to instances of unanticipated shifts may be impacted by this stress, which can also have an impact on the brain functions required to get through the school day.

Dealing with a variety of unanticipated feelings and challenging circumstances can cause problems for autistic teens that make them unable to cope.

When a teenager with autism feels stressed, their brain may activate a process that prompts a flight or fight reaction. Although the event may not seem important to those around the person, the teen with autism experiences tension and varying degrees of worry.

Difficulty recognizing Emotions

When they are struggling to deal with it, autistic adolescents go through various feelings, but they may need assistance to identify, comprehend, and control those emotions.

For instance, an autistic teen may experience all disagreeable or bad feelings of rage. Or they may not be able to tell when they are happy. They might categorize all difficult-to-describe emotions as "being bored."

Teenagers with autism might also require assistance to recognize, understand, and react appropriately to other people's feelings.

HOW TO AID TEENS WITH AUTISM IN RECOGNIZING EMOTIONS

Autistic teens may be familiar with the terms for emotions, but they often struggle to recognize them in others and themselves, especially when they're unhappy.

They might also find it challenging to read body language, tone of speech, or facial emotions in others.

Here is how to get started.

1. Identify your teen's Emotions.

Start with more uncomplicated emotions like joy, anger, and fear before moving on to more complex ones like resentment, envy, or shame.

You can tell your teen "I can see that you're angry."

Having difficulties with that instrument chord?

Then encourage your teen to explain physical feelings.

For instance, you might say it feels like a "blender in their stomach" if your kid appears anxious. Or you could mention how their pulse pumps more quickly when they are afraid.

2. Make emotional observations of fictional people.

For instance, you could view an interesting movie together and discuss how the characters' actions reflect their emotions.

It can be easier for your autistic teen to embrace their emotions if they know why they feel the way they do, and by describing to your teen how thoughts and ideas can result in emotions, you can help them comprehend why they feel the way they do.

For instance, you and your teen could sketch an image of a dog. Then you could say, "You'll feel scared if a dog leaps up at you and you think it's going to bite."

However, if you imagine what a happy, active dog it is, you might experience excitement instead.

To help your autistic teen connect emotions with ideas and behavior, you could also use cartoon strip dialogues featuring figures with a range of faces and thought boxes.

You can sketch stick figures of your teen and a companion to depict a discussion. Use various colors to convey what they are experiencing, thinking, and speaking.

Your teen must comprehend that everyone feels a variety of emotions as part of developing a knowledge of them.

You could state, for instance, "It's common to experience all kinds of emotions, like happiness, sadness, excitement, and jealousy.

Emotions can vary in size from large to tiny, and all of these emotions are normal, and it might be beneficial to discuss how strong emotions will subside with time.

Refusing to interact

An autistic teen may experience overwhelming emotions in other ways besides having meltdowns. They might also choose not to engage, retreating from difficult circumstances or ignoring them entirely.

Things to do

- Don't criticize them if they are acting out or aren't reacting to you.

For a teen with autism and their caregivers, it can mean the universe.

- Give them some time: Recovering from emotional overwhelm or sensory overload can take some time.

- Inquire about their feelings calmly if they're OK, but be aware that they may take longer to reply than you anticipate.
- Make room: Do your best to establish a calm, secure area.

Do anything you can think of to lessen the information overload. Turn off noisy music.

ANXIETY

The world can be a complicated place for teens with autism because of its uncertain character and unspoken norms, and many of them experience anxiety. If they don't have the skills and techniques to control their anxiety, they risk having an autistic meltdown.

Create a coping Strategy for Anxiety.

Prepare a strategy for what to do if an autistic teen becomes nervous and anxious, such as having a tension ball in their bag or a selection of soothing music they can listen to while out shopping.

Include some Downtime in the Schedule.

Autistic teens will typically feel relaxed and be better able to control themselves when something that might cause a breakdown happens.

It will depend on the individual what that entails. Still, it could be peaceful activities like going for a stroll in a quiet place, enjoying relaxing music, playing a game on a computer, reading an interesting book, doing puzzles, or using violin instruments. It could be more active activities like bouncing on an inflatable or going to the gym.

When engaging in more demanding activities, make sure the teen feels calmer afterward. If it doesn't, but they appreciate doing it, schedule time for that activity. However, try to find something that helps them relax so you can also schedule time for that.

HAVING COMMUNICATION PROBLEMS

When they are having trouble managing their emotions, autistic people can find it challenging to communicate their desires and needs, from a non-verbal infant who struggles with communicating their need for a drink to an adolescent who finds it tough to express their feelings.

Due to these overpowering emotions, such as rage and irritation, an autistic meltdown may occur.

Find methods to make your conversation more comprehensible and assist your autistic teen in learning how to recognize and communicate their emotions properly before they become overloaded.

Since some autistic teens can misunderstand facial expressions, tone of voice, cynicism, and humor, the vocal conversation can be challenging.

You can attempt the following:

- Social stories that are supported by visuals
- Picture Exchange Communication Systems(PECS)
- Using written information alters your vocal conversation, such as using concise phrases.
- Using technology, such as iPads, speech recognition software, instant chat, etc., to improve social and emotional intelligence.

What are Triggers is next in chapter 3.

3

WHAT ARE TRIGGERS?

Autistic triggers are physical, emotional, and mental factors that might trigger an outburst or meltdown in an autistic person.

GUIDELINES FOR IDENTIFYING AUTISM MELTDOWN TRIGGERS

Do your autistic teen's meltdowns happen at random? Good news: There is always a cause for meltdowns.

Although it can be challenging to identify the causes of an autistic meltdown, these suggestions will help you become more conscious.

Autism-affected teens often "act out" their emotions, and they communicate in a similar manner. They don't just use words to convey their feelings; they also use their entire body.

An autistic meltdown conveys, "I'm frustrated and upset, and I have no idea what caused it or what to do about it."

To assist autistic teens in communicating their emotions and uncertainty in more suitable ways, it is your responsibility as a parent to decipher these subliminal triggers.

If your autistic teen occasionally experiences meltdowns, know that it is very likely that you can find a way to comprehend those emotions while changing how they are expressed.

There is never an unknown cause or excuse for an autism outburst. Before an autistic meltdown, there are always warning signals, usually extreme stimming or fidgeting.

How to identify your Teen's Triggers is shown below.

1. Examine the influences of the surroundings on autism meltdowns.

- Have their surroundings lately changed?

Because autistic people do not habituate, they will not readily become accustomed to something over time. For instance, if the standard workstation sets in a classroom have been substituted for other seating arrangements, an autistic student is likely to suffer more during that arrangement than their non-autistic classmates.

When they enter and take longer than a few seconds to locate a spot or fall on the way there, it will be apparent that they are disturbed by the change in a sitting position.

Even their scores might suffer. Consider subtler explanations if their surroundings have remained the same.

People who are not autistic do habituate, so they are likely to miss even the most negligible differences, such as a light or new sound.

Are there any new sounds or possible distractions?

- Is there a loud commotion coming from a student at school?
- Have you recently added a plug- or battery-powered object to your home?

Often, autistic people can perceive wavelengths that non-autistic people cannot, such as electrical tones. A frequent trigger of meltdowns for autistic teens is noise.

- Have you switched your washing detergents?

They might be scratching or feeling uneasy with the new one because of their sensitive skin or the smell.

- Has their recent social interaction increased?

Their vitality may be depleted more rapidly by increased social contact, leaving them exhausted. In this case, social contact is a trigger for a meltdown.

The capacity to process sensitive information and self-regulate is reduced when emotionally fatigued. Stated they had run out of juice.

The most complicated triggers to identify are environmental triggers.

You might never discover the external cause for your autistic teen's behavior unless you are that teen yourself or they can communicate their emotions. Even if the meltdowns only occur at school, something from home may still be to blame, and vice versa.

If you cannot determine what precipitated an autistic meltdown, attribute it to external factors, and if you can, they should separate themselves from such triggers.

Take your time and look for any trends.

Keep a journal and record each action your teen engages in if necessary. Ensure you get rid of any paper records so your teen can't discover them; if necessary, burn the paper record.

2. Watch out for symptoms of sensory overload.

One of the simplest autism meltdown triggers to identify is sensory overload. More than normal, your teen will jitter or squirm.

Stimuli associated with autism should not be mistaken for Tourette's syndrome or face convulsions. It is stimming if they resemble an internet router processing data by flashing quickly.

A more forceful presentation of self-regulation is possible. They might start screaming and striking, take items off shelves at random, or try to damage property.

Direct sensory feedback and external triggers can both contribute to sensory overload. What you hear, see, feel, smell, and taste are all examples of sensory information.

3. Don't attempt to eliminate the triggers of autism meltdowns in one day.

Finding the triggers of meltdowns requires effort. You won't be able to identify the cause of the autistic meltdown by overstressing yourself.

No autistic teen desires to experience an autistic meltdown, but it can occasionally be beneficial. After everything has built up, meltdowns assist in resetting feelings, and the lethargy that follows a therapeutic outburst is a strange sensation.

As you investigate the cause of their behavior, provide a secure environment where they can recover from an autistic meltdown without feeling ashamed.

Ask your autistic teen questions like these as you converse with them about their meltdown:

- How did you feel just before it happened (meltdown)?
- Why do you believe you experienced it, exactly?
- What can you do to signal that you are about to have a meltdown from now on?

Although some autistic individuals may be able to predict when they are about to have a meltdown, they might not be able to prevent it. Expecting your autistic teen to do both is unrealistic.

4. Till it's not, assume a rage is an autistic meltdown.

Analyze each temper outburst as a potential meltdown. On the outside, every tantrum-like autistic meltdown appears to be one.

When something doesn't go their way, autistic teens struggle to control their feelings, which leads to tantrums or meltdowns, a condition of purely emotional anguish.

An autistic meltdown can occur at any moment during a rage. An autistic meltdown will intensify and last longer if handled like an outburst, and a temper outburst will swiftly calm down if you treat it like an autistic meltdown.

An autistic meltdown can commence with one of the following:

- A modification/change in plan or routine
- A violated agreement/promise
- Mistake in communication
- Feeling misled
- Feeling unheard.

- Not being able to do a thing right away or not obtaining what they've put their mind to right away.
- Efforts to appease, mainly using neutral tones and clichés. Autistic teens perceived this as a form of manipulation.
- Fake or unclear decision. For example, giving two fake choices to empower them is a form of reverse psychology and is seen as manipulation.

5. Tell the truth.

An autistic child's inability to have or do something at the moment often causes them to have a tantrum.

Delayed satisfaction is a learned skill, and non-autistic individuals are built to appreciate something more that they had to wait for, so it's more than just a learned skill. People with autism do not feel this.

Waiting for something for a long period makes autistic teens impatient and makes them lose interest. Rarely do autistic people have pastimes; instead, they have specialized interests. They lose interest in it if they cannot pursue a particular passion immediately.

People who are not autistic natural desire agreement. It is the way their minds work. They consider posing fewer inquiries, so they don't.

The minds of autistic people don't work on an obedience basis. You ignore your child's requirements if you tell them they don't need that object because you don't believe they do. By default, they cannot distinguish between essentials and desires, but they cannot acquire this skill by having someone else explain their needs.

Because it gives them such a pleasant visual stim and makes them feel at ease, that object might be a visual stim for them, and due to how delicate it is, it might also be a physical distraction. It is equivalent to telling someone they don't need to feel that way to hear that they don't need it.

People who are not autistic can infer context by interpreting hidden meanings or making assumptions based on their experiences.

For context, autistic people first look to exact language, then analyze prior encounters with every phrase or word in a statement. They never assume by responding to questions; instead, they are troubled by those queries because they frequently need more context.

To avoid offending non-autistic people, autistic people have learned to refrain from asking those questions.

Inform them why you won't buy them the gift rather than stating they don't "need" it. Even if it makes you uneasy, saying, "I don't have the cash to pay for that right now," is a legitimate justification and sufficient response.

A lack of confidence and trust results from the accumulation of little white lies and assumptions. Honesty and openness will help you and your autistic child develop a strong bond.

Use social stories to help your child bond and talk about their emotions and experiences. It will assist you in teaching your child to recognize their immediate needs and the reasons behind them. They will gain the ability to identify their triggers to autistic meltdowns as a result, and most importantly, it will give them the confidence to talk to you about those triggers.

6. Managing anger

Discussions about anger outbursts (At those moments when the child is peaceful) can help you lay a base to build on when finding their autistic triggers because "meltdown triggers" and "angry emotions" are closely linked.

Ask them some critical questions regarding their emotions. For example, what makes you sad, angry, or happy?

It is not meant to justify acting out but to teach them how to recognize different emotions and what it means to feel joyful, angry, sad, depressed, frustrated, etc.

It enables them to express their emotions to you in a way that puts you in the best possible situation to teach them coping skills.

7. Delayed gratification

The rigidity of autistic teens is typical. If they have their hearts fixed on a particular thing, they'll want it now, and if they fail to obtain it, they might lose it.

Teens with autism lack the coping mechanisms to comprehend the idea of delayed gratification. As parents, we know that "waiting" calmly for a prize or a wanted action can make it that much tastier.

As a result, you will be responsible as a parent for educating them to wait for what they want. Play pretend with them to practice this, or write a social tale about "waiting for something special."

8. Recognize bodily signs

Physical signs frequently accompany imminent meltdowns.

The child's nervous system goes into overdrive when a stimulus is present. It can result in recognizable feelings, like, rapid heartbeat, tense muscles, flushed cheeks, cold hands, rapid breathing, etc.

As they are experiencing the stimulus you are describing, ask them how they feel physically. Knowing their body's physical signals can be a natural trigger for them to put the new solution you came up with during your problem-solving talks into action.

9. Fostering individuality

Your teen can believe they are the center of the universe, and parents should always be at their beck and call to get what they want. Of course, life isn't like that, and seeing someone else receive recognition can be a significant trigger for a meltdown.

It could happen if you have a companion, additional children, or are hosting guests.

Parenting your autistic teen requires you to instill independence in them. For instance, give them a chance to relax at home by letting them play with fun and relaxing gadgets. It will frequently transfer into keeping them occupied while you're paying attention to something else, which can prevent meltdowns.

10. Internal anger

Perfectionistic and compulsive behaviors are common in some autistic teenagers.

The "meltdown engine" can start to speed up when they repeatedly try to get something right or can't communicate their ideas and feelings clearly through words.

Your most remarkable instrument for finding your child's "low frustration tolerance" is observation. Please take note of the danger signals and pay heed to them.

Pay attention when your child attempts to knot their shoes, do schoolwork, play a board game with pals, or watch a movie. Always keep your eyes and hearing alert, and keep an eye out for links and trends.

11. Over-stimulation

Even though many autistic teenagers appreciate going out to dine, shopping, visiting friends, or going to birthday parties, etc., it can become too much for them, causing them to respond to strange faces and settings. They may become frustrated due to "the unfamiliar," mainly if there are many new sounds, faces, and scents.

Therefore, you might want to "bail out" and go back home for a time out if the surroundings seem too "sensory-unfriendly" for them.

12. Parents Running around

Time is more clear to teenagers than it is to adults. They are aware of your concern about deadlines.

However, they can only sometimes move swiftly enough to satisfy your requests.

Try to determine whether there is a correlation between your constant rushing and your child's frequent meltdowns.

Of course, there will be moments when you need to move quickly, and your child must do the same. When this occurs, be explicit about your goals and take action.

For instance, you might have to nudge them to hurry if they are late, especially if they need to catch the bus. Try to accomplish this without yelling or anger. Additionally, if you feel like you are always hurrying your child with "special needs," try your hardest to calm down whenever possible.

13. Continuity of action and routine

Teenagers on the spectrum tend to depend on rituals to make them feel secure and satisfied because too much action and change can confuse them.

A significant tantrum and meltdown trigger that can quickly set off your child is a shift in routine. So, make an effort to follow your everyday schedule as exactly as you can.

If you must alter the schedule or change the routine, make sure they are relaxed and happy about it. Let them carry a beloved device or anything that helps them feel comfortable if they need to go somewhere. Take them to a tranquil area if they are beginning to show meltdown symptoms.

14. Shopping

For the majority of autistic teenagers, shopping is not a fun pastime. It might feel like a sensory attack on your child, leaving them overstimulated since sensory overload can result from the sights, noises, contact, and general "busyness" of everything.

However, if your child makes it through the sensory overload, their annoyance at not receiving everything they desire may result in a tantrum or meltdown.

Shopping with teens with autism prone to sensory overload is therefore not generally recommended. However, there will inevitably be instances when taking your child shopping is essential.

Keeping it brief would be beneficial if this were the situation. Set explicit standards and adhere to them. In this case, the best thing to do is transform your child from an inactive observer to an active partner.

You can accomplish this by assigning them a task. For example, help put the bought items into the trolley, unpack them, and choose them.

However, loading the entire cart with something for them will be easy. It is a very high bar to set for oneself.

If you go shopping with them, let them buy something independently, but you can specify what that is (for instance, their preferred cereal, ice cream, food, etc.) and then put the cap on that.

15. Transitional situations

Moving from one experience to another, such as getting up, walking to school, switching from "play time" to "homework time," etc., presents an ideal trigger for meltdowns in teens with autism.

Since autistic people dislike change, many changing situations can result in meltdowns. Autistic people struggle with change.

They may be resisting having to change instead of not wanting to take a wash or get dressed. Give your child some time to adapt when change comes about.

Of course, this is simpler said than done in a hurry-up world. But teens with autism do require more attention. For example, in the morning, they may need to stay in their pajamas for a little while before getting dressed.

Additionally, "prepare" your adolescent for changes as frequently as possible. For instance, "We're going to

Grandpa's home in twenty minutes. You can start completing your game.

SENSORY OVERLOAD

Meltdowns can also be triggered by sensory overload.

A person experiences sensory overload when one or more senses are overstimulated to the point where they become overwhelmed.

It occurs when the brain processes more sensory information than it can handle. People who are overloaded with sensory information may feel agitated, worried, or emotional. Sensory overload frequently results in pain and severe anxiety.

Sensory overload is one form of sensory processing disease (SPD). Due to either sensory hyperactivity or hyposensitivity, people with SPDs do not react to external cues in a typical manner.

When hypersensitivity is severe, a person may respond to feelings others might not even be aware of, like a fan's smell or fluttering sound.

Extreme symptoms caused by sensory overload include:

- Fear and anger
- Restlessness

- Easily irritated
- Overexcitement
- Tense muscles
- Higher pulse rate
- Breathing too fast
- Severe perspiration
- Putting something over ears or eyes to shut out the noise
- Refusing to be touched

When a sensory overload is severe, it can lead to self-destructive behaviors like head pounding, ear slapping, self-scratching, or self-hitting.

Alternative Responses

When autistic teen experiences sensory overload, they frequently mistake it for a "tantrum" or think it just happened. It is because reactions can vary from circumstance to circumstance and are not always the same.

For instance, a teen suffering from sensory overload may react differently to flashing lights at home than at school. Or, they might be immune to loud, low-pitched sounds but susceptible to high-pitched noise.

They might respond in one of the following ways:

Stimming: Repetitive actions like walking, swaying, or striking one's foot

Sensory-seeking behaviors; Smelling items or fixating intensely on moving objects are examples of sensory-seeking behaviors.

Sensory avoidance behaviors: Running away from standard images, noises, or sensations

Distraction behaviors include focusing intently on a favored feeling.

Why Does Sensory Overload Occur?

Whether an individual has autism or another developmental or psychological condition, the reform of SPDs can vary.

People respond differently to different kinds of stimulation, which can cause sensory overload. They may consist of the following:

- Sounds:

Lawnmowers, laundry machines, chiming timers, or water trickling are tenacious noises.

- Sights:

Such as a florescent light that flickers or fluttering drapes

- Smells:

Scents that are incredibly potent or distinctive, such as those from cleaning supplies, fragrances, new rugs, or cuisines

- Textures:

Consuming items that are slick or handling a sticky substance

In the next chapter, I will discuss why build coping Skills. Happy reading

4

WHY BUILD COPING SKILLS?

Each individual with autism experiences autism differently. While some teenagers will need assistance with everyday tasks and controlling undesirable behavior, others will require assistance with networking and forming positive relationships.

Teenagers who have autism gain the cognitive skills necessary to live a complete and joyful life by learning coping skills.

Examples of coping skills are exercise, journaling, meditating, and many other healthful practices. It can be something that provides them something to concentrate on other than their rushing thoughts, such as playing with a beloved object or listening to relaxing music.

Early coping skill development and exercise will help teens recall and use those skills in social situations.

Coping skills aid autistic teenagers in understanding how to behave in various social contexts, such as conversing with people or playing with peers at school.

Coping skills can assist autistic people in forming friendships, learning from others, discovering new interests, and fulfilling hobbies. Additionally, these coping skills can strengthen family ties and offer teens a feeling of inclusion.

Additionally, your child's emotional health and general quality of life depend on them having practical coping skills.

Stress is experienced by teens with autism as well. They must therefore learn stress management techniques just as much as other teenagers do. People of all ages, including teenagers, can manage stress by developing coping skills.

Teaching autistic adolescents mental and physical coping skills can help them manage the tension that comes with life's difficulties, such as academic strain and daily ups and downs.

Although they may need it, many autistic teenagers lack the social skills to seek assistance. They are still figuring out how to process their emotions, making it challenging to recognize their feelings and seek assistance.

What are some autism handling techniques and tactics I could use with my child? May have crossed the minds of parents of autistic teenagers."

An excellent place to start is for parents to be aware of when their teenagers have a meltdown or are provoked by something external.

Teaching coping skills to autistic people can help them cope with tense circumstances and prevent meltdowns that might otherwise occur.

There are many various kinds of coping skills, and only one method will be effective for some. As an illustration, some people stroll while listening to music, others practice deep breathing exercises, and others go outside and take in the scenery.

The truth is that it's critical to assist our children in identifying the coping skills that are most effective for them, and it is essential to comprehend a person's cues before you can show them coping skills for particular scenarios. For an adolescent with autism, understanding the best ways to handle nervous and tense feelings can be extremely beneficial.

COPING SKILLS FOR MANAGING EMOTIONS

Teens with ASD frequently have difficulty controlling their emotions. Big feelings in autism can be challenging to manage and communicate in a suitable way due to sensory integration issues, speech difficulties, and a lack of social signal comprehension.

Everyone affected by emotional eruptions may find them challenging. While it may not come quickly to people with autism, emotional control is a skill that can be learned.

WHY TEENS WITH AUTISM FIND EMOTIONS DIFFICULT

Autism with high functioning can be complicated. On the one hand, they have the linguistic and brain abilities to function normally. However, they lack the social, verbal, and mental processing abilities to adapt well to change.

Additionally, you might be dealing with a sensory malfunction, anxiousness, or other problems that make it nearly difficult to handle glaring lights, noisy sounds, and high demands.

People with autism frequently act out when they are extremely irritated or furious. When they do, they might act in a manner that shocks or surprises those around them.

For instance, they might:

- Meltdown with crying and yelling akin to a much younger kid.
- Run away from a challenging circumstance, sometimes risking their safety.
- Become hostile or rude.
- Overreact and be unable to control their emotions.
- Be unable to think, which, in another circumstance, would assist them in settling down.
- Become too agitated to take soothing advice.
- Display self-stimulatory actions (hand flapping, etc.)

Teens with autistic spectrum syndrome frequently—if not always—have trouble controlling their emotions and remaining composed.

They might also use other strategies to deal with some of the constraints they experience but find it difficult to express or comprehend.

Autism can occasionally be anything but "mild." It can be complicated, particularly for teens and their parents. No parent wants to witness their child in agony when something is not going well.

Teens with autism can control their emotions, though, with the proper coping skills.

ANGER MANAGEMENT

Anger is frequently a feeling connected to autistic spectrum syndrome. Most teens with autism do not show their anger in the same manner as their classmates who doesn't have autism.

The anger may be aimed at others or themself (self-injurious behavior).

Aggression from anger can take the form of striking, stomping, biting, or hurling things, and people with autism may exhibit extreme rage or violence for a variety of causes, including:

- Communication problems when expressing their needs or emotions.

- Receptive language problems, such as being unable to grasp orders or pick up on nonverbal cues from others.
- Hypersensitivity to sensory stimuli that may cause overstimulation.

Finding possible methods to deal with anger and violent actions is simpler once the cause of anger and aggression is better understood.

With the proper coping skills, like focused breathing exercises and deep breathing, adolescents with autism can successfully control their anger.

IMPROVING COMMUNICATION WITH COPING SKILLS

Unsurprisingly, many people with autism spectrum disorder (ASD) struggle with verbal and nonverbal communication since the condition is characterized primarily by impairments in social communication and interpersonal skills.

For the severity of the person's autism and the specific autism expressions that affect them, this difficulty can manifest in a variety of ways and to varying degrees. For some people with autism, communicating is as easy as it is for anyone else, while for others, it is their biggest challenge.

Some autistic individuals might find it challenging to communicate verbally. They might need help to start or keep up conversations, or their linguistic development might be postponed.

They might also find speaking nonverbally through body language, eye contact, or facial expressions difficult. Additionally, some autistic teens may struggle to engage socially or interpret socially helpful cues.

Teens with autism can enhance their communication skills with the proper coping strategies, such as using social stories and role modeling.

TAKING CARE OF SENSORY OVERLOAD

Teens with autism can learn coping skills to deal with sensory overload.

When you have more sensory information than your brain can handle and organize, it is said that you have sensory overload. A noisy party, bright ceiling lights, or multiple talks in the same space can signal sensory overload.

Anybody can experience sensory overload, and different individuals have various causes, but autism and other health problems have been linked to sensory overload.

SENSORY OVERLOAD SIGNS AND SYMPTOMS.

The signs of sensory overload differ from person to person.

Some typical signs include:

- Concentration issues are brought on by conflicting sensory information.
- Extreme agitation
- Unease and restlessness.
- The compulsion to block sensitive information with your eyes or ears.
- Excessively ecstatic or "wounded up."
- Worry or fear related to the environment.
- Increased sensitivity to materials, marks, patterns, and other objects that might brush against flesh.

WHAT TRIGGERS SENSORY OVERLOAD?

The brain operates like a sophisticated, elegant computer system. The brain analyzes the information transmitted by your perceptions and determines how you should respond.

But when there are conflicting sense data, the brain can't process it all at once.

Teens with autism may experience this as feeling "stuck" because their brains cannot select which sensitive information needs to be focused on.

Their body then receives a signal from their brain telling them to get away from some of the sensitive information they are taking in.

The body begins to fear because the brain feels imprisoned by all the information it receives. Deep breathing, walking in nature, and mindfulness meditation are coping skills that can assist with sensory overload.

In chapter 5, I will talk about the types of coping skills. Come with me.

EXPRESS YOUR GRATITUDE

By leaving a review at the end of reading this book *"Coping Skills for Teens with Autism"*, you will be providing valuable insight and information to other parents, caregivers, and educators who are seeking ways to help teens with autism.

By taking the time to leave a review, you are contributing to the online community of readers who share similar interests and concerns. Your review can spark conversations and inspire others to share their own thoughts and experiences.

5

TYPES OF COPING SKILLS

Although many coping skills exist, researchers typically identify five different coping skills. The most effective coping skills typically assist autistic people in confronting their stressors rather than avoiding them.

There are, however, some outliers. Furthermore, healthful practices carried too far can be detrimental.

1. FOCUSED PROBLEM-SOLVING SKILLS

The quickest way to relieve stress is to take immediate action to address an issue. It works better when teenagers cope with a particular and manageable case or circumstance rather than general worry and anxiety.

Coping skills that are problem-focused include:

- Enquiring as much as possible about the circumstance, including the individuals who can help you find a remedy.
- Dividing the issue into doable parts and tackling each piece separately.
- Developing the necessary coping skills to handle the signs and symptoms associated with the condition (autism)
- Identifying triggers, stressors, and any other problem that can cause tantrums or meltdowns.
- Applying coping skills in dealing with the daily challenges of autism.

2. EMOTIONAL COPING SKILLS

Not everything that happens to us or around us causes stress. Stress can be the outcome of internal processes.

Autistic teenagers' perception of stress and worry dramatically influences how they respond to their ideas and emotions. Below are two emotional coping skills for teenagers to manage their autism.

Practice Breathing and Relaxation

Teens with autism today experience higher levels of worry and anxiety than other teenagers. They must therefore learn how to calm and relax.

Relaxation skills offer helpful ways to manage stress and lessen the likelihood of autism meltdowns. They, therefore, stand a higher chance of averting negative coping strategies like drug misuse and self-harm.

As a result, scientists are advancing new studies on integrative and natural calming methods. These efficient options for medicine are also being provided to young people by clinicians and other medical experts.

YOGA FOR AUTISM.

How does yoga help teens with autism?

According to research, yoga's focused breathing and exercise trigger a calming reaction.

Thus, yoga helps to exit the autonomic nerve system, also known as "fight or flight." As a result, we enter the parasympathetic nerve system, also known as the "rest and digest" system.

Additionally, practicing yoga raises GABA levels. The chemical in the brain that promotes mental relaxation is called GABA.

Participants in a 12-week trial alternated between an hour of yoga or walking thrice weekly. More significant rises in GABA levels were seen in the yoga group, and they also displayed more considerable reductions in worry and depression.

Yoga is, therefore, among the most crucial calming techniques for Autistic teenagers.

A calming yoga exercise

A straightforward yoga position renowned for promoting calm is the child's pose. So it makes for a great calming technique for teenagers.

How to perform the Child's Pose.

- Bring your pelvis down toward your feet while on your hands and knees.
- Keep your big toes in contact while separating your legs widely.
- Embrace the summits of the legs with the midsection.
- Lay your midsection on your legs and place your face on the floor.
- Knees may be joined or separated.
- Put your arms out in front, palms down, or lower them back to rest next to your legs,

palms up.
- Slowly inhale for five counts, then slowly exhale for five counts.
- As long as you like, continue to hold the position.

DEEP BREATHING EXERCISE

One of the most effective relaxation techniques for teens with autism is deep breathing, and one of the simplest and fastest methods to calm the nervous system is conscious, regulated breathing.

We enter the parasympathetic nervous system's rest reaction as we breathe more slowly. Consequently, one of the best calming methods for autistic teenagers is deep breathing.

Deep breathing exercises are an effective way to unwind before exams, settle down when angry or worried, and fall asleep more quickly.

The breathing process makes room for calm and focuses on the psyche.

Studies on teen breathing exercise.

By research, breathing techniques are proven practical, effective instruments for relaxing the nervous system. Additionally, these calming methods produce results quickly.

For instance, in a study conducted in 2016 by researchers at the Medical University of South Carolina, 20 healthy individuals were split into two groups. One group then completed two rounds of ten-minute deep breathing routines. The other group spent 20 minutes reading a book of their choosing simultaneously.

Researchers periodically examined the participants' spit while engaged in these tasks.

The findings revealed that three particular cytokines had significantly reduced amounts in the sputum of individuals who engaged in the deep breathing exercise. Stress is linked to these cytokines.

Researchers concluded that there was a quantifiable reduction in worry and stress due to the deep breathing exercise.

RELAXATION EXERCISE

Square Breathing Exercise

Four-square breathing or box breathing are other names for square breathing.

Autistic teenagers can use this deep breathing exercise as a go-to calming technique.

How to do Square Breathing Exercise

- Sit comfortably in a chair with your feet flat on the ground and your hands on your knees.
- Allow air to enter your abdomen with a steady, four-count nasal breath.
- Hold the air for four counts.
- Count to four while steadily exhaling through the mouth.
- Imagine a refreshing blue or whitish radiance flowing over your body as you breathe.
- Finally, retain the air for four counts.
- The process should be repeated four times.

Ideally, perform the practice four times a day for four minutes each time. Performing square breathing regularly will make autistic teenagers calm and more at ease.

MEDITATION

According to research, mindfulness-based activities like meditation can lower anxiety, stress, and anger. Additionally, they raise the quality of life and emotional health.

Meditation is crucial for autistic teenagers as a method of rest. And the research found that meditation is more beneficial than travel for boosting calm and mental health.

Two sets of 90 individuals each were drafted for this research, and seasoned meditators conducted this research. Additionally, a group of people who had never meditated participated in the study.

The first group participated in meditation, while the second group didn't practice meditation. Instead, they spent a week engaging in enjoyable holiday activities while listening to health talks.

Everyone then felt more at ease. However, researchers checked in with the subjects again 10 months later.

And they discovered that worry and stress levels significantly decreased in regular and novice meditators. However, the ones that went on vacation had leveled off and were back to their pre-vacation stress and worry levels.

Therefore, it is evident that meditation has a solid and enduring effect on worry and stress.

Simple Mindfulness Meditation Exercise

Here are instructions for a brief meditation that can be introduced to an autistic teen's repertoire of stress-relieving techniques.

- Close your eyes and take deep breaths while you sit silently.
- Draw focus on your breathing.
- To help maintain mental concentration on inhaling and releasing, say the mantra "breathing in, breathing out" several times.
- Acknowledge an idea as "a thought" and allow it to pass through your consciousness like a cloud moving across the sky.
- After that, slowly return your focus to your breathing.
- You can practice for as long or as little as you like.

Even a brief period of meditation can have a profound impact on your day and attitude.

Teens' Relaxation Technique: Music

Researchers have discovered that calming and relaxing music significantly affects the neural system. Stress and worry are improved considerably by listening to calming and relaxing music.

As a result, music promotes intense calm in teens with autism. Rhythm serves as the governing force for all of the cells in our body, and they all work in unison.

Rhythm is what regulates our respiration, sleep pattern, and pulse. We can enhance regulation or down-regulate the neural system because our bodies naturally react to exterior cadence.

Autistic people don't need to rely on things or drugs from outside to be calm and relaxed. They can accomplish the same goal without negative consequences and more effectively with soothing music.

Studies with sad teenagers revealed that music therapy altered their brain activity and cortisol levels (the "stress hormone"). Researchers concluded that music had calming impacts on their physical and mental capacity.

Music therapy helps autistic people feel less frustrated, angry, and aggressive.

Spent time outdoors in nature.

Spending time outdoors improves relaxation, and an increasing collection of studies supports the idea that autistic teenagers can benefit greatly from spending time in nature outdoors.

Japanese forest bathing is where this area of research got its start. In experiments on "forest bathing," some subjects were taken into the woods while others were taken to cities.

Afterward, they took the subjects' cortisol, blood pressure, pulse, and heart rate variability readings. As a result, they discovered that in comparison to cities, forest bathing generated less cortisol, a better heartbeat, a lower heart rate, and more autonomic nervous system activity.

The research thus demonstrated the obvious advantages of spending time in nature for stress relief.

Positive Visualization

Positive visualization increases an autistic teen's ability to relax. Meditation and positive visualization are effective techniques for releasing mental and bodily stress.

Teenagers who engage in positive visualization exercises learn to control their emotions and manage stress better. As a result, it is one of the best calming techniques for teenagers.

"Visualization taps into a universal awareness of ourselves and our feelings, bypassing our rational (or erroneous) thinking. It enables us to recall positive emotions or to encourage a feeling associated with particular situations.

RELAXATION THROUGH BODY SCAN VISUALIZATION.

- Locate a quiet, private area and sit or lie down in a relaxed posture.
- Take a few steady, deep breaths while you are closing your eyes.
- Imagine being in one of your special places—a lovely spot. It could be a quiet area of the seashore, the forests, your home, or the home of a loved one.
- Consider your surroundings in your mind's eye. Think about the sound of the ocean or the breeze in the treetops.
- Feel the sun's warming on your skin or the ocean's refreshing wash.
- Continue to imagine the scenario, taking in every detail.
- Remember that you can return here whenever you want or need to unwind.

Autistic teenagers can benefit greatly from this visualization strategy when feeling stressed, distracted, or agitated. It allows them to exercise self-awareness and concentrate on deliberately resting their bodies to settle their minds.

MAKING MEANING

Using meaning-making techniques, teenagers can alter their perspective of a stressful circumstance. We can alter how we feel about a challenging circumstance by trying to see its good or essential parts.

We have two vital areas to examine under "meaning making":

1. Reframing
2. Journaling

REFRAMING

Teens with autism can view a circumstance, a person, or a relationship from a more wholesome perspective by using reframing to help them change their attitude and point of view.

Self-critical ideas and judgments frequently go through the minds of teenagers. That makes sense, given how challenging puberty is.

At this age, they work hard to develop their self-worth, create identities, and make friends outside the family. They will inevitably encounter difficulties and have self-doubts during this turbulent development time.

It's normal to think negatively; it's a form of survival. Our early predecessors used a genetic process known as "negativity bias." People were more likely to survive a tiger assault or a storm if they gave careful attention to warning indications of peril.

Teenagers are therefore predisposed to overlook the positive events that also occurred, such as receiving praise, having fun with friends, or receiving an embrace from a loved one, in favor of focusing on the adverse events, such as failing an exam, receiving a critical remark, or missing a soccer goal.

However, these negative thought patterns can ultimately result in mental health problems like depression, anxiety, and feelings of rage and despair. So, reframing unfavorable ideas is crucial for promoting adolescent mental health.

Autistic teenagers who use reframing techniques can escape the tendency of pessimism and develop new, more optimistic perspectives on the world and their selves.

What is Reframing?

One of the most successful cognitive behavioral therapy (CBT) methods for teenagers is reframing, also known as cognitive reframing or cognitive reworking.

The fundamental tenet of cognitive behavioral therapy is that our thoughts and feelings are interconnected, with our feelings influencing our actions. As a result, altering our thinking also affects our emotions and actions.

Therefore, cognitive reframing can assist teenagers in changing their mentality and point of view so they can view a circumstance, people, or connection from a more positive angle.

They can alter their unfavorable ideas by reframing them, which will change how they perceive a circumstance and, in turn, how they feel and react to it.

By reframing unfavorable ideas and thoughts, they can:

- Turn their attention away from the drawbacks of a circumstance and toward its advantages.
- Alter skewed perceptions of events or individuals.
- Have a better understanding and analysis of what they're going through
- Be mindful of their mental processes.
- Examine the integrity of their negative assumptions.

How Negative Thought Reframing Affects Mental Health.

Pessimism and prejudice are no longer in our best interests. In reality, catastrophizing, or ruminating about all the possible adverse outcomes, harms our health and well-being.

Teenagers who use cognitive reframing can escape the tendency of pessimism and develop new, more optimistic perspectives on the world.

One research, for instance, discovered that teenagers who practice positive reframing could better rethink social circumstances, which might be especially beneficial for teenagers with social nervousness.

Reframing can also be a successful strategy for autistic teenagers who are having difficulties with the following:

- Anxiety
- Low self-esteem
- Depression
- Eating problem
- Insomnia
- Abusing drugs
- Problem with social interaction
- PTSD
- Stress and worry

The Benefits of Positive Self-Talk and Cognitive Reframing for Autistic Teenagers

Teenagers frequently internalize their bad thoughts as negative self-talk, and they often severely criticize themselves and assume that others do the same rather than being sympathetic champions for themselves.

Cognitive reframing teaches people how to speak to themselves with love and empathy. Adolescents' self-esteem and self-confidence can be raised by using this CBT method.

Autistic teenagers who practice positive self-talk teach their brains to focus on their assets and strengths rather than their faults and issues. For instance, they can change "I'm terrible at XY" into "I'm still learning to do XY" using optimistic self-talk (Reframing).

They could also say instead of "I messed all up," "I see what didn't work well, and I can do it differently next time."

One way of brain reframing is called the ABCDE strategy:

A: Stands for the active trigger for unfavorable ideas.

B: Stands for the Beliefs that cause destructive emotions.

C: Stands for the causes or emotions the triggering incident brings.

D: Stands for disputing or challenging these false ideas.

E: Stands for changing one's thoughts and emotions about the triggering incident.

Six Effective Ways to Practice Reframing Negative Thoughts with Autistic Teens

Teenagers with autism can feel more powerful and optimistic by reframing unfavorable ideas and circumstances.

Here are some suggestions for teaching them to engage regularly in cognitive reframing.

1. Assist them in recognizing negative thought patterns.

Teenagers frequently think negatively, which causes them to assume the worst-case scenario or the worst possible decision immediately.

They can become aware of their routines and inclinations through writing, meditation, and discussing their ideas. The first stage in changing negative thoughts and habits is to recognize them.

2. Pose inquiries.

Socratic inquiry is a technique that helps people reframe unfavorable ideas and thoughts.

Try asking questions like:

- "What other angles might you approach this?"
- And "What information or proof do you have to back up your claims?"

Teenagers considering these issues may become aware that they are overreacting or catastrophizing.

3. Assist them in getting a broader perspective.

Remind your child of the broader perspective if they draw unfavorable or illogical inferences. For instance, a loss can be reframed as a chance for development and learning.

4. Discourage the use of absolutes.

Teenagers frequently have an all-or-nothing perspective on the world, seeing only good or evil, right or wrong. But, with cognitive reframing, they will identify the intricacy and murky areas in any given circumstance.

5. Remind them that life isn't all about them.

Autistic teenagers frequently overthink situations and place the responsibility for unavoidable circumstances on themselves. But, realizing that much of what happens in their environment has nothing to do with them can be a tremendous source of comfort for them.

6. Pay attention to triggers.

Teenagers frequently go through a lot of pain because they assume what other people will think or that a specific circumstance will turn out badly. But, with reframing, a pessimistic teen with autism may be able to look at things more positively by focusing on the best-case scenarios rather than the worst-case scenarios.

JOURNALING

Teens with autism who journal can better understand their emotions and see their experiences as part of a broader narrative.

How Journaling Can Increase Happiness

Expressive writing or journaling has numerous beneficial effects on health and well-being, particularly when practiced regularly.

Here are a few ways that journaling is suitable for your emotional well-being.

- **Emotional**

It aids in worry and stress management. You can spot external stresses and determine internal issues by writing about what's causing anxiety and stress. And occasionally, you need to let it all out, even if it's just on paper.

It raises the mental quotient. You can better understand and make meaning of your emotions by writing about how you're feeling.

Enhanced Communication abilities. Learning to communicate and express verbally to others correlates with writing your ideas and thoughts on paper.

- **Personal**

It aids in goal-setting and achievement. With journaling, your brain will be informed that your desires and goals are significant and will move one step closer to becoming a reality if you write them down. In addition, verbalizing our ideas enables us to organize tasks and requirements.

It encourages self-control. It makes it easier to adhere to a routine when you write daily, even when you're not in the mood to. As a result, you're better equipped to perform other tasks that call for self-control.

It aids in fixing problems: Journaling helps us see things from new angles without looking for answers, enabling us to consider a circumstance from various angles.

- **Increases Empathy**

Writing about a situation or connection enables you to understand better what other people may be experiencing or thinking as you engage with them. It increases our awareness of our routines and trends.

- What brings you joy?
- When do you feel the most anxious?

Reviewing our writing over time can help us determine what contributes to or hinders our well-being.

- **It boosts imagination.**

Writing enables us to develop our creativity off the paper and in other spheres of our lives. We also develop the ability to think outside the box regarding handling suffering, challenging feelings, and problematic relationships.

These advantages accumulate over time to mitigate the signs of melancholy, anxiety, and other adolescent mental health illnesses. Writing, in general, makes us happy.

How to Begin a Journal

- Are you prepared to start your own creative diary or writing practice? Use these basic instructions as a starting point.

Pick a diary or writing technique:

- What equipment suits you the best?
- A notebook with a lovely cover and your preferred pen?
- A piece of paper and a mechanical pen?
- iPad or laptop?
- Select the strategy that appeals to you the most.

Locate the proper location.

- Find a place or places in your house where you can relax, have some solitude, and aren't constantly interrupted or bothered by commotion.

Choose a period that usually works:

- Determine the time of day that you typically write.
- Early in the day before class?
- The evening?
- When there is a natural pause in activity in the middle of the day?

Try to compose at that time each day, or at least most days, even if only for a short while. Experts recommend 20 minutes per day.

Spelling, syntax, and punctuation are unimportant:

Let your ideas run efficiently onto the paper or computer without critiquing your presentation.

Whether to share it or not

Some people find that speaking aloud from or allowing others to read their journals is a beautiful way to express their emotions.

You have an option; whichever you make, you'll enjoy all the beautiful advantages of journaling.

In the next chapter, I will discuss the different types coping Skills for Autistic Teens. Let's go.

6

COPING STRATEGIES FOR AUTISTIC TEENS

Teens frequently experience anxiety and stress with an autism spectrum disorder.

In this chapter, I'll review some relaxing techniques that can help teenagers on the autistic spectrum feel less anxious and more relaxed.

These strategies include breathing exercises, methods for visualizing things, meditation, and awareness exercises.

People with autism may experience meltdowns for a variety of reasons, and stress or worry is one typical reason.

People with autism may struggle to cope and feel overloaded when nervous or agitated, which might trigger a meltdown. Sensory overload, change in routine, anger, and exhaustion may also bring meltdowns.

Teen autistic meltdowns can greatly upset them and their parents and caretakers. However, some strategies can aid in calming down and reducing meltdowns.

People in the autism spectrum can benefit from a variety of soothing techniques that can help them manage their anxiousness and encourage calm and relaxation.

One effective strategy is giving the teen a location to go to when they're feeling stressed, and they can unwind and relax in this private space.

You can assist them when they need to withdraw by turning down the lights, lowering the volume of sounds, and supplying a comforting item or activity.

DEEP BREATHING EXERCISE

One of the best strategies for handling anxiety and stress is deep breathing. The body can become calm and relaxed, and the pulse rate can be slowed with deep respiration.

Deep breathing techniques can be a beneficial method for teenagers with ASD to relax and lower stress levels.

Practicing deep breathing is an excellent method to encourage calm and lessen worry.

Diaphragmatic breathing, or abdominal breathing, is one deep breathing practice that can be beneficial.

To perform this activity, put one palm on their tummy and the other on their torso.

The next step is for them to inhale deeply through their nostrils while enabling their belly to rise.

After a prolonged, full inhalation, they should gently let it out through their mouth.

How to Perform Deep Breathing Exercises

- Draw a long breath in.
- Then Let it out.
- You can also count from 1 to five as you inhale, then 1 to 5 as you exhale

You might already have noticed a change in how you feel. Your exhalation can reduce anxiety and relieve stress, and you'll notice a significant improvement if you incorporate some easy breathing techniques into your daily regimen.

Before you begin, bear the following in mind:

- Pick a location where you can practice breathing. It might be in your bed, the living room floor, or a cozy recliner.
- Avoid pushing it. You might become more anxious as a result.
- Try to perform it once or twice per day at the same time.
- Put on relaxed clothing.
- To reap even more considerable advantages, perform them for 10 minutes or longer when you have more time.

Most individuals inhale quickly and shallowly into their chests and might become nervous and lose energy.

Using this method, you can take deeper breaths into your abdomen.

- Become at ease.
- With a cushion under your head and legs, you can lay on your back on a mattress or the floor.
- Alternatively, you could recline in a chair with the top of the seat supporting your neck, head, and shoulders.
- Breathe in through your nostrils.

- Allow air to enter your stomach.
- Utilize your nostrils to exhale.
- Put one palm on your stomach.
- The other palm should be on the chest.
- Feel the stomach expand as you inhale.
- Feel the stomach drop as you exhale.
- Compared to the hand on the chest, the one on the stomach should move more.
- As the stomach raises and descends with each inhalation, you deeply breathe into it.

BREATHE FOCUS

- Use a mental image and a term or sentence to help you feel more at ease as you take long breaths.
- If your eyes are open, shut them.
- Breathe in deeply for a few moments.
- Inhale deeply, and imagine the air is infused with tranquility as you do this. Try to experience it all over your body.
- Breathe out. Imagine that your worry and anxiety are released into the air as you do it.

Use a statement or sentence while breathing out.

Say to yourself, "I breathe in peace and calm" when breathing in.

Say to yourself, "I breathe out stress and tension" as you exhale.

Keep going for ten to twenty minutes.

EQUAL BREATHING TIME.

Breathing in and out. You will synchronize the length of your breaths in and out during this practice, and the ability to hold your breath for more extended periods will gradually improve.

To do this

- Take a seat in a recliner or on the floor.
- Inhale through your nostrils. Count to five as you do it.
- To the count of five, exhale through the mouth.
- Repeat some times.
- Increase the time between breaths once familiar with the five breathing counts.
- You can eventually breathe for up to 10 seconds.

PROGRESSIVE RELAXATION OF THE MUSCLES.

In this method, you inhale as you contract a muscle area and exhale as you relax it. Your bodily and emotional rest is aided by progressive muscular relaxation.

To do this

- Lay down on the ground.
- To feel relaxed, take a few long breaths.
- Inhale deeply.
- Your feet's muscles should be tensed.
- Exhale.
- Relax your feet and tensed muscles.
- Inhale deeply.
- Pull in the leg muscles.
- Exhale your breath.
- Calf tightness should be released.
- Move up your torso in steps.
- Tense all muscles. It includes your fingertips, limbs, shoulders, neck, cheeks, thighs, abdomen, and torso.

MINDFULNESS

Another effective strategy for controlling autism-related anxiety and stress is mindfulness. Focusing on the here and now while remaining objectively aware of our thoughts, emotions, and experiences is called mindfulness.

By bringing about a feeling of serenity and focus, mindfulness can aid in calming an autistic person.

With mindfulness, autistic teens can concentrate on breathing as a proper awareness exercise. They should take a slow, deep breath through the nostrils, followed by a slow, deep breath through the mouth.

They should only pay attention to their breathing and nothing else. Mindfulness can be performed as required for a few minutes throughout the day.

How to Practice Mindfulness

It only takes a few minutes per day to exercise mindfulness techniques. The fundamental stages are as follows:

- Take a comfy seat.
- Choose an object to concentrate on, such as your breathing or a phrase you keep repeating to yourself.

- Say you choose to concentrate on how you are breathing.
- Give focus to the breath while continuing to breathe regularly.
- You have the option to shut your eyes.
- Please pay attention to each inhalation as it is taken in and out.
- Pay attention naturally, on purpose, but not obtrusively.
- Keep track of any times your thoughts stray from concentrating on your breathing.
- Consider what you're having for lunch, whether you bring your sports equipment, that amusing story someone made after math class, or other things.
- That is your thoughts straying and becoming preoccupied.
- That's what brains naturally do all the time.
- When you become aware that your focus has strayed, softly direct it back to your breathing.
- You maintain your focus in this manner.
- Continue to breathe, unwind, and give casual attention to your breathing.
- Every time your thoughts stray, keep returning them to your breathing.
- Try to maintain this for five minutes.

Mindful Walking

In this practice, you'll take a leisure walk while paying attention to how your body moves.

- Start by picking up one foot and moving it slowly forward.
- Concentrate on how you manage yourself effortlessly.
- Now move slowly, one stride at a time.
- Take note of the motions of your ankles, thighs, and limbs.
- As you slowly raise one foot, then the other, pay attention to how your legs flex and stretch.
- Time your inhalations and exhalations with your movements.
- As you unwind and breathe, try to concentrate and be deliberate with your steps.
- When your thoughts stray, softly nudge them back to your slow, deliberate movement.
- Remember to keep inhaling in and out as you appreciate going in slow motion.

Mindful Word

Consider a term that evokes tranquility or comfort. Such a term might be "peace," "love," "peaceful," "snowflake," "sunlight," "hum," or "calm."

- Consider the phrase silently. In your mind, utter them slowly and in silence.
- Repeat the phrase to yourself with each inhalation you breathe, both in and out.
- Keep the calming phrase in the center of your concentration.

When your thoughts stray, bring them back to your word and continue to utter them slowly and softly as you unwind and breathe.

- Can you maintain this for one full minute?
- Do you have five minutes to spare?

EXERCISE

Studies have shown that teens with autism can reduce repetitive behaviors, restlessness, and hostility by engaging in intense exercise for more than 20 minutes.

Exercise not only improves social interaction in autistic teenagers, but it also aids in weight reduction and improves general health.

Full-body exercises are ideal for them to improve balance, muscle, endurance, and bodily awareness.

Try these five exercise routines.

Advice for beginning

Instructing them in a new activity in a relaxed and encouraging setting is crucial. Use encouraging words like, "You're doing a wonderful job!"

Additionally, use vocal or physical signals to direct them through the motions and lessen the likelihood that they will become irritated or angry.

1. Bear stoops

Bear movements promote the growth of bodily consciousness, enhance muscle planning and synchronization, and strengthen the upper and midsection of the body.

How to do this:

- On all fours, place your palms under your shoulders and your legs under your pelvis.
- Legs should be extended and slightly bowed.
- To make the most touch with the surface, spread your fingertips widely.
- Cross the floor with your hands and feet about 10 to 20 feet.
- Holding this posture, move rearward in the same manner.

- For best outcomes, try varying the direction and pace.

A parent or instructor can offer hands-on assistance at the pelvis if the exercise is too challenging.

2. Slammed medicine ball

Weighted item throwing, such as with medicine balls, can strengthen the core, balance, and coordination. It can also activate the brain regions in charge of short-term memory and may have medicinal advantages.

How to do this:

- Stand with a medicine ball in each palm.
- Straighten your wrists as you raise the object aloft.
- With all your might, slam the object to the floor/ground.
- Repeat the motion 20 times while bending your legs to gather the object.

You can make this practice more difficult by tossing the ball to strike a goal or making the ball heavier.

3. Star Jumps

Jumping activities are excellent full-body workouts that strengthen the legs and midsection, enhance body awareness, and improve aerobic stamina. Star jumps are simple exercises that can be done anywhere, either one at a time or repeatedly.

How to do this:

- Start crouching with your legs bowed, your feet level on the ground, and your arms at your torso.
- Quickly rise from the floor and form an X with your arms and knees.
- Return to the beginning posture after landing with your arms and knees curled.
- Continue until you become tired after up to 20 rounds.

4. Arm movements

Authors of research published in Autism Spectrum Disorders discovered that motions resembling those made by autistic individuals might aid in giving the body the input it requires. It might lessen repeated actions like applauding or flailing arms.

An excellent upper-body exercise that improves strength and flexibility in the shoulders and back is arm movement, which can be performed anywhere without special tools.

How to do this:

- Arms by your side, ankles shoulder-width apart.
- At shoulder height, extend your arms straight out to the side.
- While maintaining your arms erect, start creating little loops with your palms.
- Increase the size of the rings gradually as you rotate your shoulders.
- Do it twenty times, then move oppositely and continue.

5. Mirror drills

Difficulty engaging with others or the surroundings is a common feature of autism.

Mirror activities urge the teen to imitate what another individual does, which can improve their balance, self-awareness, and social skills.

How to do this:

- Hands by your side, face your companion.
- Ask your companion to start moving their limbs slowly.
- Start with circles and work your way up to more intricate designs.

- When you're set, imitate the other person's motion as though gazing into a mirror.
- For instance, you raise your left if they lift their right arm.
- For additional input, try gently brushing your palms.
- For one to two minutes, keep doing this.
- Consider including the head, torso, and extremities as additional bodily components—three to five times.

Pro advice

Before beginning a fitness program with a teen with autism, always contact a doctor.

Start slowly and keep an eye out for symptoms of exhaustion like loss of breath, tightness in the muscles, or vertigo. Before starting, make sure the adolescent is well-rested and refreshed. It's ideal to begin moderately and gradually increase to more demanding, intense practices.

To sum up

Teens with autism can profit greatly from exercise. According to research from Developmental Medicine and Child NeurologyReliable Source, a sedentary lifestyle can exacerbate the mobility disorders that affect 79 percent of autistic children.

Exercise has been shown to boost happiness, better coping skills, improve quality of life and reduce harmful behaviors.

VISUALIZATION

Another effective technique for encouraging calm in teens with ASD is visualization.

Visualization entails creating soothing, serene pictures in mind. Doing so can divert from stressful or anxious thoughts and emotions.

Techniques for visualization can also ease worry and encourage calm. One visualization method is to ask them to picture a serene area, like a seashore or a field.

They should pay attention to the little things in this serene setting, like the scent of beautiful flowers or the sound of the seas. This practice can be performed as required for a few minutes throughout the day.

MUSIC

Music is a creative art that ranges from serene and soothing to quick and energizing. Everyone can find something in music.

Many autistic individuals seem attracted to music because of its soothing and healing qualities. Music can help individuals cope with a tense or unpleasant task by calming them down just enough to get them through it.

TAKING A LEISURE WALK.

More and more people are becoming aware of the numerous advantages of walking outside or in nature.

Some individuals who are a little more active—like those who have been identified with autism—might require some exercise to focus. The person may require a stroll outside to relax and feel energized.

The autistic teen may need to escape from a stressful setting by taking a stroll outside, where vegetation and other natural elements are anticipated, to complete lessons in a stressful classroom.

DO SOMETHING ENJOYABLE AND RELAXING.

These activities may embrace, but are not restricted to; one's favored pastimes, reading, sketching, or anything else that makes one happy. Knowing and doing something enjoyable is soothing and relaxing for the autistic individual when things are problematic and seem overpowering.

ACTIVITIES FOR COPING WITH AUTISM IN TEENS

Yoga

Advantages of Yoga for Teens with Autism

Teens with ASD frequently struggle with verbal and receptive speech, sensory integration impairments, and social/emotional difficulties, including trouble comprehending and identifying others' facial expressions, social signals, and feelings.

They can display a wide variety of behaviors in these areas, with some having more trouble than others in one or more, and many might also struggle with increased stress and worry.

Yoga has recently attracted attention as a potential remedy and extra support for teens with ASD.

Increased psychological and social abilities, communication and language abilities, body awareness, self-management, focus, and concentration, as well as a decrease in anxiety, impulsive, irrational aggressive, and self-stimulatory behaviors, have all been noted as benefits of yoga in addition to the usual ones like increased strength, balance, coordination, and flexibility.

1. Improved social communication skills

One study's findings, published in the International Journal of Yoga Therapy, suggested that copying skills can improve with yoga.

The research found that teens with ASD may profit from yoga as a helpful instrument to improve mimicry, cognitive abilities, and social-communicative behaviors.

They also showed improved eye contact, seated endurance, non-verbal speech, and sensory communication abilities.

The growth of social-communication skills is closely linked with the capacity to comprehend one's actions and replicate them. They acquire yoga postures and breathing techniques by mimicking the actions and mannerisms of the adult when performing the poses and breathing techniques.

Additionally, it helps them maintain shared focus, which can be difficult for teens with ASD.

The growth of communication and language can also be aided by visualization, direct imaging, and a repeat of words with the help of visual tools and pictures.

2. Understanding and expressing emotions

Yoga practice can increase awareness of social skills in teens, such as their feelings and how they feel, as well as their actions, behaviors, and facial expressions.

Due to their frequent struggles with vocal and receptive speech, people with ASD may communicate their feelings surprisingly or improperly.

With yoga, teens with ASD can learn breathing techniques to help them express challenging or unpleasant feelings like rage, irritation, or worry in healthier and more positive ways.

Giving them a means of actively expressing their feelings sends the message that experiencing those emotions is okay and can help them feel better mentally.

3. Reduced Stress

Many autistic teens have higher stress levels. It may impact their health, behavior, temperament, and sleeping pattern.

They may experience continuous anxiety due to speech difficulties, sensory processing impairments, and a variety of other problems.

The fight or flight response is commonly used to describe this nervous condition. Their intellect and speech decline when they are in the fight-or-flight response, and they frequently start deep breathing or hyperventilating, making them feel even more anxious.

With yoga, it is possible to teach specific breathing techniques to help individuals with ASD cope with worry and calm their nervous systems.

They can develop coping skills, self-control, and better physical and mental reactions to stress with the help of focused breathing, guided images, and relaxing postures.

Better sleep, metabolism, temperament, behavior, and general health and well-being are all supported by calming their nervous systems and letting go of any stress in their bodies and thoughts.

4. Decrease in Difficult Behaviors

People with ASD often exhibit demanding behaviors due to the many challenges they experience in speaking and speech, mood expression, maintaining focus, and sensory integration.

The American Journal of Occupational Therapy recently researched the relationship between yoga and behavior improvement. A substantial effect on the behaviors of teens with ASD was observed when assessing problematic behaviors before and after the yoga intervention.

According to the study's findings, autistic teens who performed yoga regularly for 16 weeks demonstrated behavioral improvements.

Combining breathing techniques with yoga postures can help children with ASD reduce worry, which harms mood and behavior, and helps them learn self-control and coping mechanisms.

Teens with ASD frequently struggle with visual coordination "Sensory integration" describes how our systems use and handle internal and exterior cues from the world around us.

Self-regulation is the capacity to plan one's activities, manage one's degree of awareness, and manage one's emotional, mental, or bodily reactions to stimuli. Attitudes, demeanor, activity level, and reaction to external cues are all impacted by self-regulation issues.

To promote sensory integration and self-regulation, specific postures and breathing techniques can be taught to individuals with ASD. These techniques provide proprioceptive and vestibular feedback from the two "hidden" sense systems. The improvement of impetuous, combative, and acting-out behaviors can be significantly seen with the development of self-regulation skills.

5. Higher Body Awareness

There is a chance that many people with autism have poor bodily awareness, and they can better understand their bodies by learning about them through yoga and physical exercise.

Body consciousness is also supported by poses that offer proprioceptive and sensory feedback. A better feeling of bodily consciousness can be attained by understanding the directional ideas taught in yoga, such as up and down and left and right.

6. Positive Self-esteem

The practice of yoga can aid individuals with ASD in building self-confidence and self-esteem, in addition to the numerous advantages mentioned above.

For teens with ASD to practice, balancing postures and standing poses especially are fun and effective.

Any position, whether standing, swaying, or sitting, can be altered to support the child's ability to boost their self-esteem and make them feel accomplished.

Teenage yoga practice while standing.

As you start your practice, remember that yoga is an exercise of the body and mind.

Except for the leaps, proceed leisurely and pay attention to the present.

Here are some basic guidelines and directions to bear in mind before you start:

- Choose between chest-to-abdomen breathing and concentration.
- For eight to ten breaths, hold each position while breathing.
- Repeat the entire procedure on both surfaces twice.
- It should take 15 to 20 minutes to complete this process.

When you're prepared, perform the standing exercise as follows:

- Take the peak pose to begin.

- Start your preferred method of yoga meditation.
- Jump or step into an overall posture with your arms in a T position horizontal to the floor as you exhale.
- Turn your feet and body to the right and lift your arms from the sides as you breathe.
- Sink into the warrior I pose, bending your right leg to a 90-degree angle as you release.
- As you inhale, adopt the Warrior II posture by turning your shoulders to the left and dropping your arms into a T with your hands facing down.
- Open your rear (left) shoulder as far to the left as it will go, then easily curl your leg under.
- For the first variant of the reverse triangle, turn your shoulders to the right and bring your left and right arms horizontally to the floor as you exhale.
- With your right knee still bowed and your head turned to the right, take a deep breath in, and then, as you exhale, lower your left hand to the floor and raise your right arm straight up.
- Turn your head downward if your neck starts to hurt.
- Roll down with your arms, torso, and head as you exhale. Then, with your feet straight and

hanging down the center, extend your legs forward while holding on to your forearms.
- Jump or stride back into the mountain position after rolling your torso up.
- On the left, repeat Steps 1 through 9.

Teenage yoga mat practice.

Since achieving wide-legged sitting forward bends without natural hip flexibility takes a lifetime, some people refer to this exercise regimen as the Lifetime Sequence.

The appeal of yoga is that, even if you don't succeed at first, you can get it right next time.

Here are some pointers to bear in mind before you start:

- Opt for a chest to abdomen breathing or concentration.
- Hold each position for six to eight breaths (including when you lift your arms).
- Repeat the entire series twice.
- It should take 20 to 25 minutes to complete this task.
- Every one of the forward bends is appropriate for softening your knees.

- Don't overburden yourself; instead, push yourself.
- This exercise is not advised for those whose lower back pain is made worse by rolling.

When you're prepared, perform the floor exercise as follows:

- Start with your spine erect and your limbs in the air.
- Take a forward lean to your sitting position as you breathe.
- As you breathe, straighten your spine, lift your arms to shoulder height, and spread your thighs widely.
- Bend down and forward to a spread-legged forward bend as you breathe.
- As you breathe in, as you did in Step 3, lift your limbs and torso to a straight-back posture.
- Exhale, turn to the right, and lean down and forward.
- Like in Step 5, lift your limbs and torso to a straight-back posture as you breathe.
- Turn to the left, lean down and forward, then exhale.
- Put your heels up, flex your knees halfway, and lift your arms and torso to an erect back

posture as you breathe.
- Try to move your legs down as you breathe and lean forward and down.
- As you breathe in, straighten your limbs and back while bringing your legs to your sides and fusing the bottoms of your feet in tandem.
- Hold your ankles while bending forward and down as you breathe.

Teenagers with autism need to be actively involved in a variety of activities if they are to learn and develop skills that would otherwise be difficult for them to achieve.

Their confidence, sense of value, and overall well-being can all be improved by engaging them in activities like yoga, arts and crafts, singing, caring for animals, and even playing video games.

15 COPING ACTIVITIES FOR TEENS WITH AUTISM

1. Playing board

Children with unique needs, including those with autism, can benefit greatly from playing board games, and autistic teens can learn difficult-to-master skills like focusing, adhering to norms, and taking turns by playing board games.

Please ensure the board game's degree of challenge matches your teen's skill when selecting one to play with them. It would be best if you started with a straightforward game like Dominoes, ludo, or Snakes and Ladders, where you only have to roll the dice and move the figure.

Chess and other more complex strategy games might be enjoyable for your teen if they have strong visual-spatial skills. Some board games, like Social Skills Bingo for teenagers, emphasize teaching social skills, questioning techniques, and body language awareness.

2. Painting

Painting can be a fantastic medium for adolescents with an autistic spectrum disorder to communicate themselves, and studies show that participating in creative pursuits helps autistic people to express their thoughts and emotions.

Painting and sketching are two activities that can help your autistic teen improve their fine and large motion and visual-spatial skills. Additionally, they positively influence social skills, dialogue, and self-esteem.

Utilizing the Draw Something application is something you can recommend if your kid enjoys technology. It is a social sketching tool that lets adolescents communicate with peers and email drawings. With its wide range of tools, sketching options, color effects, and backdrops, the Scribblify coloring software can be another entertaining way for teens with touch sensitivity to create art.

3. Exercising

Teens with autism frequently have weaker muscles and poorer balance, which can all impact their everyday living skills and self-esteem. Regular exercise will enable them to appreciate a range of activities with peers and family and better their bodily health.

In addition to enhancing learning and social conduct, physical exercise can also help to mitigate stress and anxiety and improve overall well-being.

In teenagers with autism, regular physical exercise has been shown to reduce repetitive behaviors like body swaying, stimming, and head bobbing.

4. Cooking

Cooking is a calming and reliable pastime perfect for teens with autism. Meal preparation is a vital everyday skill that will help them become more autonomous as an adult.

Preparing meals and dining together are fantastic ways to improve social skills.

Consider sensory problems, movement limitations, and dietary intolerances before teaching your autistic teen how to cook.

5. Reading

Every autistic teen's daily regimen should include reading because it fosters language development and enhances learning and cognitive skills. Please encourage them to read a range of easily understandable fantasy, academic, and science works and books written primarily for teenagers with autism.

6. Watching TV

A well-planned TV schedule can help them develop information and abilities that will be helpful in both the classroom and outside of it. For instance, they will be able to develop the social skills required to debate a range of subjects with their classmates through game shows and films.

Additionally, certain TV shows can teach them appropriate behavior in a variety of scenarios and foster social skills.

7. Video games

Because of their graphic elements, organization, and quick input, video games frequently appeal to teenagers with autism. Playing video games can help them because it promotes the growth of logic and reasoning abilities and inventiveness, and originality.

MMOs and multiplayer games are great resources for enhancing your teen's social skills. Among the video games your adolescent might like to play are New Super Mario Bros., Portal 2, and Minecraft.

8. Puzzles

Teens with autism benefit greatly from puzzles because they provide a physical experience while fostering their concentration and fine motor skills. Additionally, solving puzzles can improve their thinking and imaginative skills and help them feel less anxious.

Solving problems with others can improve their speaking and conversation skills.

Constantly pick a piece challenging enough for your autistic teen, and urge them to discuss their progress as they work on it.

9. LEGO

Teens with autism often enjoy playing with LEGO pieces. Since the available block forms and sizes are restricted, and the construction process necessitates repeated motions, the activity is considered organized and dependable.

For teenagers who struggle with social anxiety, such as when engaging with people they don't know well, building with LEGOs can be helpful.

According to studies, when autistic teens play with LEGOs frequently, they become more involved in engaging with one another.

Children are encouraged to use vocal and nonverbal communication skills, share, learn how to take turns and problem-solve while engaging in this type of play.

10. Domestic duties

Doing domestic tasks is one of the best methods for autistic teenagers to grasp ideas like accountability and sharing. Start them with easy jobs like placing items back where they belong, feeding plants, or picking up mail from the letterbox.

You may instruct them on more complex duties as they become accustomed to doing them, like making the bed, arranging the table, tidying the home, or preparing a basic dinner.

11. Music

Music has a powerful affective impact on many autistic teens, and rhythmic noises frequently hold their focus much longer than spoken words do. Another effective multi-sensory activity that can help your autistic adolescent develop their speaking and social skills is listening to music.

Furthermore, music boosts confidence and provides protection and comfort.

Taking music lessons and instrumental performances are ways they can enjoy the soothing effect of music. Enhanced mental well-being and cognitive ability are the outcome of stimulating the brain to create new links and enhance old ones through music.

Additionally, it might assist them in developing balance, focus, rhythm, fine motor skills, and inventiveness, and participating in a singing group can help them develop social and speaking skills. They might appreciate learning and performing the guitar, violin, piano, trumpet, and bongos, among other instruments.

12. Dancing

The enjoyable activity of dancing can significantly impact the growth and development of teens with autism. Joining a ballet class can be incredibly helpful for developing your child's focus and recall, speaking skills, sensitivity, and capacity for adaptation to various circumstances.

Their body image and bodily consciousness will both improve from dancing.

13. Meditation

Controlling the interaction of their thoughts and bodies is a significant struggle for many autistics. The critical areas teenagers with autism battle, like cognitive skills, sensory problems, and social interaction, can be addressed through meditation.

It can help them focus on the current instant rather than allow their feelings to control them. They will learn how to relax with the help of guided meditation applications such as Headspace, Calm, or My. Life, which was made especially for teenagers.

14. Animal Care

According to research, individuals with autism who engage with animals behave much more socially. Your autistic teen may benefit from the company of animals and reduced anxiety and stress.

Having a companion will help them develop accountability and empathy. Older pups or young dogs, guinea pigs, bunnies, pet rodents, and fish that your child might find calming to gaze at make the best pets for autistic teenagers.

Of course, having a companion is not a requirement for them to care for animals. They can engage in a variety of animal-related activities, including equestrian riding, working with animals at a nearby farm, helping at wildlife centers, and adopting cats or pups.

In chapter 7, I will discuss how to cope with autism while at school. Happy reading.

HOW TO COPE WITH AUTISM WHILE AT SCHOOL

Teens with autism may experience difficulties studying and having fun at school. And they may exhibit certain behaviors.

Working with schools is essential to helping them with their worries about education.

Strategies consist of:

- Practicing and becoming acquainted.
- Relaxation and expert assistance.
- Identifying the causes of worry about education.
- Identifying the causes of school stress.
- Working with schools to reduce worry and stress in teens with autism.

- Practice and education techniques for reducing school anxiety
- Supports and visual aids for reducing classroom anxiety.
- Techniques for identifying emotions and settling down.
- Support from professionals

Teenagers with autism may experience school anxiety for many of the same reasons as normal growing kids. For instance, classrooms can be crowded, loud environments with lots of people around.

There are exams and tasks. Additionally, schedule disruptions at school can leave them wondering what will come next.

However, it's also normal for them to experience higher levels of school anxiety than others.

Your autistic child's ability to appreciate and learn at school can be impacted by anxiety at or about school. They might even lose interest in or be unable to attend school.

To assist them, it's crucial to collaborate with their education. Planning can help them move to secondary education more smoothly and with less worry.

SIGNS OF CLASSROOM ANXIETY

You may notice indications, such as an uptick in problematic behavior if autistic teens are anxious about attending school.

They might:

- Have tantrums or more than-normal meltdowns
- Desire to spend more time alone
- Depend more heavily than normal on their habits
- Depend more on routines
- Develop sleeping problem

You might observe these issues at home, or a school staff member might contact you to let you know they have noticed these or other behavioral changes at school.

Causes of School Anxiety

For teens with autism, the following are typical reasons for school anxiety:

- Being cut off from home
- Dread of school-related issues.
- A new modification at school or home.

- The responsibilities of speaking and interacting with others at school.
- Fear of academic failure.

Collaborating with the school to handle school anxiety.

Working with the school is vital in helping your autistic teen if they experience anxiety at or about school.

Staff members at the school will thus be able to:

- Describe behavior at school in more detail.
- Describe what they believe might be causing the anxiety at school.
- Describe current coping skills for students who experience worry at school and how your child might benefit from modifying these coping skills.

You will be able to communicate details about the following:

- Particular anxiety symptoms and indications in your child.
- Techniques you employ at home to calm your child.
- Anything in your house that could be causing the anxiety.

So, schedule an appointment with the school first. Their school teacher, other staff members who deal with your child, and the school psychologist or counselor could all be invited.

You could also speak to your child's student support group (SSG) if they have one. Your goal is to understand what is causing the anxiety at school. You can devise methods to support your child once you and the school personnel are aware of the circumstance.

You may need to communicate with the school frequently, perhaps daily, if your child suffers from school anxiety.

Having a primary point of communication is beneficial. It could be an instructor in the classroom, a school psychologist, or a counselor, and if you keep in touch with this individual, everyone will always be aware of how your child is feeling.

STRATEGIES FOR FAMILIARIZING ONESELF AND PRACTICING FOR SCHOOL ANXIETY

You can acclimate them to the school before they enroll in any school if they are worried about beginning school. You could go there a few times and practice the commute to school.

The stepladder method is another way to practice walking to school, and it can help some autistic teens get over their anxieties and issues.

Supports and visual aids for reducing classroom anxiety.

You can prepare them for changes in patterns at school by using pictures, visual aids, social tales, or a picture book. They may use applications to access schedules, trips, and school plans.

Because they can readily see and comprehend their habits and feel in charge of them, this can help to lessen their school anxiety. They may also benefit from visual techniques for overcoming separation anxiety at school.

You could, for instance, display a picture of:

- Themselves at school, so they are aware of their location

Techniques for identifying emotions and calming down.

Teach them to recognize the bodily symptoms of worry, anxiety, and other negative emotions. For instance, their hands start twitching, their fingers sweat, and their pulse rate increases.

They can learn the symptoms of anxiety and the circumstances that make them feel apprehensive by using an inventory of these emotions.

Consider rendering the criteria as a bodily sketch for an individual. They can use this document at home, school, and other locations.

When they are able to identify their emotions of anxiety, stress, and worry, they may attempt breathing techniques or muscular calming techniques to help them stay calm and relaxed.

Some teens benefit from massage therapy and relaxing sounds. Ensure they are aware of a secure spot at school to go to if they are feeling stressed.

Support from professionals and teens struggling with school anxiety.

Your teen must have a confidante at school. Discuss with them and the school personnel who they would feel at ease approaching for assistance. The school counselor could be in charge of this.

Using expert help outside of school is another smart move. For instance, a psychologist may employ cognitive behavioral treatments to assist your teen in learning how to modify their thinking in nervous circumstances.

HELPING YOUR TEEN TO COPE WITH AUTISM IN THE CLASSROOM

For any teen, switching classes, grades, or schools can be distressing, but for those with autistic spectrum disorders, managing worry about uncertainty can be particularly challenging.

You can lessen these worries by taking baby measures to acclimate them to their new environment before the start of the school year.

The following tried-and-true advice can assist autistic teenagers in making a seamless transfer to school and assisting them in beginning a new school year effectively.

1. Talk regularly with them about what to anticipate in school.

Talking with them is the most uncomplicated advice but is crucial for calming them down.

2. Mark off the days on your planner.

The start of the school year may cause anxiety. Your teen might comprehend the beginning of the school year easier if you mark days off the schedule.

3. Before the new school year begins, establish a new daily regimen and put it to the test.

Start acclimating them to the new wake-up time before the momentous first day by getting them up early each morning. Do a few "run-throughs" near the conclusion of the summer break so they are prepared for the time leading up to returning to school.

Create a pictorial plan detailing everything from getting ready to board the bus if they react well to them.

4. Visit the school (*For new schools*)

Even though you might not meet your child's new teachers at this early stage, they will at least become accustomed to the location and environment before going.

Visit the main office, restrooms, canteen, gym, library, field, and any other areas they might spend time in during the upcoming school year while you walk around the school. Take photos during your trip to create a social narrative so you and your child can reflect on it.

Loud sounds and changes in habits are challenging for many autistic children.

If feasible, have a school teacher demonstrate to your teen where to go and what to do in case of an emergency while on your trip. It could assist them in being ready, and it might be enjoyable to watch you walk along quietly.

5. Make a regular plan for the school year.

Even if you go through the motions, one day may help your kid feel more at ease, even if you don't know the precise pattern.

If at all feasible, request that the school teacher obtain the current school year's timetable before your visit so that you can plan your stay at the school around it.

6. Have your kid meet the teachers before the start of the school year

Remember to snap a picture of them and post it to your social account.

7. Your child's skills, flaws, potential sensory issues, nutritional limits, and preferred coping skills should all be listed in a paper.

Involve them in writing this, as their feedback will be very helpful to the teachers.

Include a few amusing and distinctive traits about your child. The teachers, assistants, and other staff members who interact with them at school should receive a duplicate of what is written (one to two pages in length).

Remember to include the director, deputy principal, vocational therapy, speech therapist, physical therapist, music teacher, etc., in your report draft. Before teaching your child, instructors find that having a "snapshot" of them is very useful.

8. Make sure a behavior strategy is in place from day one, if suitable.

Ask that a strategy your child has been using be shared with their new instructor and put into action right away when the school year begins. Make sure that every key person in the school is acquainted with the augmentative communication teen employs, if any.

Before school starts in the autumn, the instructor should be acquainted with the gadget.

There should be a strategy and training for every assistant who will work with them, ensuring that they are confident using the gadget within the initial stages of school.

9. Make sure a beloved sensory tool is accessible from the first day if they struggle with sensory problems.

The certain calming tool can provide a lot of solace for autistic teens who battle with sensory overload. Make sure they always have access to at least one.

10. Meet with the bus driver.

The final week of the summer break is when many bus drivers train. To help them feel at ease taking the bus to school, request a "meet and greet" with the driver.

Some bus drivers will even agree to let you and your child travel to school so that you can try that.

11. Keep track of your child's development after the school year starts.

In the first few weeks of school, get in touch with every teacher teaching your autistic teen. It allows you to monitor your child's development and communicates your interest in and commitment to your child's achievement to the school personnel.

12. Thank the school management on behalf of your teen in writing.

It never harms to express gratitude to those who contributed to your child's seamless adjustment to school and learning activities in school.

13. Please offer to help.

Your school attendance demonstrates your commitment to your child's education. Additionally, most pupils enjoy seeing their parents at school. You will receive points just for showing up.

14. Try to relax

Autistic teens are able to sense their parents' stress. Your ability to control your stress will help them remain more composed throughout the school year.

Handling Autism in the Classroom

How to Address Behavior Issues

Teens with autism frequently express their demands, fears, and complaints through their actions.

These actions may include:

- Fidgeting
- Stimming
- Rocking
- Tapping
- Repetition of sentences or words
- Mimicking
- Self-destructive behaviors
- Aggression
- Neglecting friends.

- Refusing to adhere to instructions.
- Eloping

Some habits can interfere with learning in a school environment, even though they are useful communication tools.

Teens with autism are taught new skills through a variety of treatments that enable them to establish appropriate communication, social, and functional patterns.

STRATEGIES FOR HANDLING CLASSROOM BEHAVIOR ISSUES ASSOCIATED WITH AUTISM.

The following strategies assist school employees in effectively managing the behavioral difficulties displayed by autistic students in the classroom.

1. Observe Your Behavior Plan.

Each autistic teen is different, so they all require a distinct behavior strategy.

A behavior analysis serves as the foundation of a behavior modification strategy to identify the behavior of autistic teens.

This analysis pinpoints the causes of behaviors, including a child's need to acquire a thing, engage in an activity, feel something, flee from a demanding or unpleasant situation, or attract attention.

The behavior analysis will characterize the prevalence and severity of behaviors, pinpoint their root causes and results, and make recommendations for potential remedies.

A special education or behavior expert creates a BIP (Behavior Intervention Plan) using data from behavior analysis.

The BIP outlines the problematic habits, their root causes, and practical remedies tailored to the child's needs. The BIP has quantifiable goals that the instructor and other staff members can keep an eye on. As the pupil accomplishes objectives, the BIP can be changed.

2. Include interests and strengths.

Every autistic teen has strengths and interests. These resources can be used as an incentive to encourage them to pay closer attention in class, remain on task, and behave better.

Discover the unique qualities of an autistic teen by paying careful attention to them.

To encourage good conduct, school employees can integrate the student's skills and interests into the curriculum and incentives program.

3. Maintain clear routines.

Many teenagers with autism may experience worry when their everyday routines change. These students may engage in inappropriate behaviors when faced with unpredictably occurring circumstances at school because they rely on regularity and constancy.

Stress and strain may be reduced by improving everyday planning and classroom framework. Children may feel calmer, less tense, and less restless throughout the school day with rituals, regular daily schedules, visible activity schedules, physical limits, and other changes.

4. Set and describe reasonable expectations.

Most teenagers perform better when they are aware of their responsibilities and can live up to them. It is particularly true for autistic teens with a very precise and tangible way of thinking.

To lessen autism-related behavioral issues in the classroom, carefully establish reasonable standards and clearly describe those expectations.

For instance, instructors might have to give straightforward directions and demonstrate to students what they need to do. Have them reiterate the directions to the instructor/teacher to guarantee comprehension and prevent tantrums.

5. *Transitions in time.*

Moving between courses and activities frequently can aggravate autistic people.

They typically enjoy regularity, dependability, and the chance to complete one task before going on to another. Time changes carefully and limits interruptions to prevent behavioral problems.

Written or pictorial plans make standards clear, and vocal cues can encourage students to make a smooth shift.

6. *Address Sensitivity Issues.*

People with autism may experience difficulties with sensory sensitivity to sounds, smells, strong lights, and materials. The distress and pain brought on by this sense of hypersensitivity may preface problematic behaviors.

To increase comfort, address their sensitivity issues. By watching the child and speaking with the parents or other caretakers, teachers can learn about the child's sensibilities.

While it may not be feasible to eliminate all of the environmental sensory issues, making small adjustments like turning down the lights or avoiding congested passageways can have a significant impact.

7. Provide a quiet, calming area.

Students with autism frequently experience unease, stress, or anxiety at school, and when they experience these emotions can lead to complex actions.

If there is too much noise in the classroom, students can unwind in a peaceful area in a nearby room or the classroom. Tools that promote their feelings of security, comfort, and safety should be in this area.

A swing, rubber wall, painting materials, dim lights, no commotion, and other tools let an autistic teen unwind and get ready to return to the classroom effectively.

8. Improve Communication Skills.

Some people with autism may profit from methods that teach practical communication skills because they frequently battle to communicate. Teens with autism may be able to speak more effectively and exhibit fewer behavioral issues in school with improved communication skills.

9. Apply calming strategies.

The staff may retaliate in kind if a pupil acts aggressively or disruptively in class, whether orally or bodily. However, maintaining composure effects and frequently diffuses rather than intensifies the situation.

When classroom personnel uses relaxation methods on themselves and the students, they can better manage challenging behaviors.

Stress-reducing techniques include deep breathing, counting to 10, having a break, pressing against a wall, and speaking slowly and quietly.

As each student builds useful instruments that encourage serenity, peacefulness, and calm, these and other soothing methods can be used immediately or integrated into the class's daily routine.

In Chapter 8, I will show you the effective ways of Coping with Autism in Social Environment. Meet you there.

8

COPING WITH AUTISM IN SOCIAL ENVIRONMENT

For autistic teens to cope in social environments and interact with people without having anxiety and meltdowns, they need to develop social interaction skills.

SOCIAL INTERACTION SKILLS FOR TEENS WITH AUTISM

Social interaction: What is it?

Understanding social expectations is essential to social engagement, which includes engaging with others. To do this, one must heed societal knowledge, understand what is happening in these circumstances, solve some problems, and then react.

For teens to effectively engage with others, a wide range of skills is necessary. These skills generally grow over time until adulthood, when they appear to connect naturally.

Most people depend on their ability to communicate with others to get through their day. Making new acquaintances, establishing connections of all types, learning from others, and discovering new hobbies are all made easier by learning how to engage with others.

It's crucial for parents of autistic teenagers that their children's interactions are built on inclusion and understanding, regardless of who they socialize with.

For teenagers, this involves figuring out how to share games, play cooperatively, or take shifts. It may entail comprehending emotional and social signals, such as knowing how to start a discussion, knowing what to speak about in specific circumstances, or being conscious of nonverbal social exchanges, such as queuing up at the grocery store.

Possessing social interaction skills also means:

- Understanding how to handle situations where you don't concur with someone or are furious or how to handle issues in your interactions at school.

- Having good social skills that help you communicate effectively.
- Participating in team activities, having a social pastime, or venturing into social settings without feeling excessively worried, apprehensive, or angry about what to anticipate.

Commonly used social interaction skills include:

- Play skills

Like sharing, collaborating, and taking turns, cooperating.

- Communication skills

Including understanding what to say, how to say it, and using body language.

- Mood management

Like controlling emotions and comprehending others' emotions.

- Problem-solving skills

Like understanding context, resolving conflicts, or making choices in a social setting.

These social interaction skills usually grow over time, but for individuals on the autistic spectrum, play and other social contact abilities frequently evolve differently, and people with autism may believe everyone else was born with a hidden instruction handbook.

The effects of Autism spectrum syndrome on social interaction skills.

Having trouble with social contact, deciphering other people's behavior, and understanding what to say or how to conduct themselves around others is a prevalent topic for those on the autistic spectrum.

When it comes to social interaction, people on the autistic spectrum will have a range of preferences, and teens with autism spectrum disorders may show little desire to engage with those around them.

Social contact may be challenging for teens in the autism spectrum, which may affect their capacity to:

- Begin or continue a discussion.
- Recognize nonverbal signals such as facial emotions and body language that provide context for what is being said.
- Make eye contact and keep it.
- Discuss a topic that is unrelated to their area of interest.
- Comprehend languages that are not precise, such as irony, slang, and analogies.
- Recognize when people use language to mask their emotions or words in a manner that obscures their intended meaning.
- Observe details that others might miss. Some individuals on the autism spectrum have extreme attention to detail and can hear every leaf move in the breeze or draw links that others can't.
- They are tactile sensitive and might find handshaking or large gatherings upsetting.
- Observe how others perceive things.
- Adapt relationships to the social or natural setting, for instance. Compared to classmates or schoolmates, behavior when engaging with elders changes.

Social contact difficulties for some autistic individuals can cause worry or a sense of loneliness. Unfortunately, more studies than any other form of impairment show that individuals in the autistic range are more likely to experience abuse.

If an autistic teen has trouble interacting with others, you can encourage them to practice by:

- Jointly playing video games
- Performance acting,
- Modelings, such as using videos and instructions
- Direct instruction in social abilities.

DEVELOPING PLAY SKILLS

Playing games with teddies or toys like tea parties, taking the bus or train, going shopping, playing card or table games like Connect Four or Uno, throwing a ball to each other, or working together on a crossword project are all ways to develop play skills.

Using a social story will help your teen prepare for having a friend over by giving them information about what to anticipate and suggestions for activities and topics to discuss.

Solving societal problems with visual aids, such as dealing with leftover cake, handling a conflict, or reacting to someone who is wounded, angry, or tired.

Use role-playing or modeling to show your kid various social scenarios and how to handle them.

Developing Social Interaction through Play Skills.

Play skills are one of the effective ways that autistic teens learn social interaction and how to cope in a social environment.

Different abilities are required for handling social interaction in a gathering of individuals compared to managing social interaction one-on-one.

Parents and experts can assist in the improvement of a child's play skills. Naturalistic teaching, also known as teaching at the moment, organized playgroups, counseling, or remedial programs can all be used to meet this need.

Early intervention clinicians, psychologists, and speech pathologists can frequently help with play skill development. And understanding their cognitive strength can be essential when helping them build play skills.

When practicing play skills, it's essential to make sure they are having fun, to play with someone they feel safe around, to take the time to make sure they are not getting agitated when you try to participate in or contribute, and to practice play skills at your child's level, for example. On the ground.

Less recognizable people may be used, and encounters may be expanded once they feel more at ease. Prompting and reward are frequently used to support the development of awareness and play skills.

Individual Play.

It occurs when a young person engages in independent play with play gadgets while actively attempting to prevent engaging in play with others. Try the following methods to increase their capacity for being able to communicate with others:

When they are playing, get near them and try to get their focus. It includes acting similarly to them or imitating their vocalizations.

An illustration would be to repeat "toot, toot" while pushing a locomotive down a track. Try to participate if they are doing something, for instance. Try to add one if they are piling blocks.

Play with a favorite object of your child's and talk to them when they come over. Use the phrases "let's play" and "good playing" to promote the notion that playing is something you do.

Group play

It is when they engage in cooperative play with other people while using an object like a railway or pail and shovel. They may briefly pay attention to other children playing before turning back to their item or activity.

To help them learn to understand and comply with basic commands and requests, encourage social play through shared focus, turn-taking, and various methods of playing with objects.

Following are some tactics for group play:

- Encouraging them to "look what they are doing" while watching other children play.
- Presenting chances for playing games and activities that require players to take turns in an organized manner, such as crossword puzzles, Potato Heads, and Jack in the Box, with vocal cues like "my turn," "your turn," etc.
- Please encourage them to ask others for toys and other things by giving them vocal or nonverbal cues.

Social or cooperative play

Children engage in cooperative play at this time, showing interest in the action and the other people participating.

Please encourage them to show that they can collaborate with others and need to socialize.

Cooperative and friendly play techniques include:

- Dividing work into manageable pieces that have a defined beginning and end.
- Supplying framework, such as visible cues.
- Promoting decision-making abilities
- Parents and caregivers can set an example for their children by using phrases like these when they are playing. Can I join your game? Will you join me in a game?
- Promoting and demonstrating the phrases "Annie's turn" and "your turn."
- Urging collective focus "What are they doing?"
- The gradual expansion of social organizations in number.
- Gradually lengthening social interactions.

Giving them a plan of both organized and free playtimes will help them develop their decision-making skills.

When individuals on the spectrum lacking social interaction skills approach adulthood, it can become more difficult for them to "fit in" and feel like a community. Even though social meetings and celebrations can help people develop their abilities, they can also make them feel stressed or anxious.

It's important to keep in mind that not just adolescents with autism deal with these situations, and if it makes them feel miserable or uneasy, try not to push them into too much social contact.

A short time of social contact may be enough for some teens with autism, and this should be honored.

SOCIAL SKILLS DEVELOPMENT FOR TEENS WITH AUTISM

Numerous social skills strategies can be employed at any age to improve social awareness and foster social skills.

These consist of the following:

1. Groups for Structured Social Skills

For teens with autism, numerous varieties of organized social skills programs are available. They are frequently used in small groups, with one clinician or another who has received training in social interaction guiding the group.

They might be provided in high schools, colleges, or the larger community. They are usually organized and use guidance or urging as necessary to assist students' success concerning the activity's goals.

Others put more of an emphasis on talent development, while some, like Lego, have a passion for concentration.

2. Social stories

Social narratives are stories that provide instances of suitable reactions and emphasize pertinent signals to explain social circumstances in some depth. Social stories are tailored to the person's requirements and are usually brief, with or without images or other visual tools.

Teens with autism can benefit from social stories to improve their social skills, better understand and interact with others, and remain secure.

Social stories can be helpful in a variety of situations, including learning self-care techniques like brushing one's teeth or saying "thank you," as well as behavioral strategies like what to do when you're furious or how to deal with compulsive thoughts.

Additionally, social stories can be helpful in the following:

- Describing how others might act or react in a specific circumstance

- Fostering awareness of the viewpoint of an autistic individual
- Dealing with regular shifts and upsetting, unplanned occurrences like a teacher's absence, a move, or a terrible storm
- Provide a person with comments on a skill or accomplishment to boost self-esteem.

Social stories function by simplifying and literalizing information. They can clarify "executive functioning" and what happens after a sequence of actions or movements. These activities can help teenagers with autism feel less anxious and more at ease.

3. Visual Aids

Picture cards, photographs, quick movies, colored cards, gauges, and line sketches are all visual aids.

Visual aids can take many different forms. Additionally, visual cards can be used as cues to help someone acquire a new ability or have a discussion.

As an illustration, consider what occurs when you go out to eat: you arrive at the eatery, interact with the serving staff, peruse the menu, place your order, the food is prepared and brought to you, you at the food, pay the tab, and then you depart.

Visual aids simplify situations so that some autistic individuals find them unthreatening.

Visual aids such as picture cards are great for visualizing and describing complex social and emotional ideas. It can assist autistic teens in recognizing the anticipated social contact in various contexts.

4. Modeling

Modeling is portraying a positive behavior that your child will learn and emulate. When a parent, expert, or friend exhibits a desired behavior, the student may imitate that behavior. It is known as modeling and may result in acquiring new abilities.

Modeling is frequently used in conjunction with other techniques like asking (e.g., "my turn") and reward (e.g., "Good taking turns."

5. Video modeling

Video modeling is the same as traditional modeling, but rather than performing the skill in real life, footage of the skill is captured on video. It allows the teen to examine the video whenever it is convenient for them and to watch it repeatedly to build proficiency in learning the skill.

There are various kinds of video modeling; some use classmates or professionals to produce the video, while others use video of the student themselves to demonstrate the skill or a portion of it, which is then put together.

HOW TO TRAIN AUTISTIC TEENAGERS TO ACT CORRECTLY IN SOCIAL SETTINGS.

With the help of parents, educators, and tutors, autistic teens can learn how to act correctly in social situations, and they can learn to engage with others socially appropriately with the right assistance.

It can be challenging for parents of autistic children to know how to educate them on how to act correctly in social situations, but some things can be done to assist them in learning this vital skill.

It's essential to keep in mind that teenagers with autism frequently struggle to comprehend social signals. It implies that they might not be aware of when they are acting unacceptably.

Because of this, it's critical to be explicit and let them know what is anticipated of them.

Please continue reading to learn how to assist autistic teens in learning how to conduct themselves appropriately in social settings.

Since every child is unique and will call for a different strategy, there is no right way to educate autistic teenagers on how to act correctly in social situations.

However, some strategies can be helpful.

1. It's critical to realize that teens with autism might not always be conscious of or comprehend societal conventions and standards.

It implies that they require specific guidance on acceptable behavior. For instance, it might be necessary to teach them how to maintain eye contact, communicate in different situations, stop when speaking, and talk at a reasonable level.

They may also benefit from visual assistance, such as social stories or using pictures for illustration, and they may gain a better understanding of societal norms.

2. Making social events as sensory-friendly as feasible is a crucial factor.

Too much commotion, brightness, or activity can be overpowering for many autistic people and make them restless or stressed out. Try to choose a peaceful area for social meetings, or at the very least, give them access to headphones or earbuds in case they become too noisy.

3. It's crucial to keep in mind that every child is unique, and what works for one may not necessarily work for another.

It's crucial to exercise patience, flexibility, and a willingness to test out various strategies until you discover one that works for your teen. It can help them handle everyday actions they might take in social situations.

Common social behaviors of teens with autism.

For parents and caretakers, some typical actions that autistic teens may display in social situations can be challenging.

- Tantrums or meltdowns.

An autistic teen may throw a fit or meltdown if they feel stressed in a social situation, and parents and other caretakers may find it extremely challenging to handle this.

- Another typical behavior is stimming.

A person with autism will do this when they sway, twirl, or wave their hands repeatedly, and because of this, they may appear unusual or disturbing to others.

- Avoidance.

When a teen with autism attempts to completely evade social contact, this is what happens, and it cannot be very pleasant for parents and other caretakers who want them to socialize with others.

How to handle those inappropriate behaviors.

Even though these habits can be difficult, there are methods to support autistic teens in adjusting to social situations.

1. Establishing a defined plan.

Teens with autism may feel more at ease in social situations if they follow a defined plan and pattern.

2. Providing visible tools

Teens with autism can better grasp social expectations with visual tools like social stories. For instance, you could write a social story about what they should do at a friend's birthday celebration.

They will be better able to comprehend and keep in mind what is expected of them.

3. Offer assistance and compassion

Children with autism may feel more at ease in social settings if their parents and caregivers are gentle and understanding.

How to control socially improper conduct and make your teen more socially acceptable

Here are some things to remember when a teen with autism exhibits inappropriate actions in a social setting:

1. Try to determine WHAT is causing the action:

- Is the kid feeling uneasy or overpowered?
- Is there a situation occurring that is causing a reaction?

You can start managing the behavior once you determine what's causing it and help to locate a peaceful area to escape the stimulus if feeling overstimulated. A peaceful place, a calming room, or even a brief trip outside might be appropriate.

It's crucial to explain to them that they are not in danger and need respite. And apply a coping strategy to help them calm and relax. It could be as easy as taking a few slow breaths or having a short break.

It is crucial to teach them that they can control their emotions and decide how to respond to a circumstance.

2. It's critical to maintain composure and patience in every situation.

Children with autism frequently detect when someone is irritated or furious, which can make things worse. Reassure them that you are there to assist them by offering encouragement and support.

Common difficulties that parents and other adults who care for autistic teen encounter when teaching them social interaction skills.

Teaching social interaction skills to autistic children can be extremely difficult for their parents and other caretakers.

Typical difficulties include:

- Identifying the particular actions that should not be used in social situations.
- Teaching fundamental social skills, such as how to smile, make eye contact, and carry on a discussion.
- Assisting them in comprehending and adjusting to other people's responses to their stimming and autistic mannerisms.

- Finding the ideal ratio of demands and assistance in social settings.

How to approach those difficulties.

Since every autistic teen is different, there isn't a one-size-fits-all approach to socialization. However, the following essential advice might be helpful:

1. Begin modestly and increase steadily.

Not all social interaction skills should be taught at once. Start with one or two fundamental skills and progress from there.

2. Follow a step-by-step process.

Divide each skill into doable, little stages. For instance, if you're trying to teach your teen how to welcome people, you might start by teaching them how to establish eye contact before saying good morning.

3. Use graphic tools and specific illustrations.

People with autism spectrum disorders may have trouble grasping complex ideas. Therefore, it can be advantageous to demonstrate what you're instructing with practical instances and visual tools.

For instance, if you're teaching communication skills, you might role-play with them or use a social story to demonstrate how to communicate effectively.

4. Be persistent and patient.

Learning new abilities requires patience and practice. So when they take even the smallest positive moves, be gentle with them and give them recognition.

It's crucial to set clear standards and then stick to them and make sure you follow through on any commitments you make.

5. Enlist the help of others

Getting assistance and guidance from others who are in comparable circumstances can be beneficial. For parents and other caretakers of autistic teens, numerous communities and support organizations are available online.

How to make sure your child can learn and develop in social situations

Since autistic teens frequently have difficulty comprehending and adhering to social norms and training them to act correctly in social situations can be difficult.

Because of this, it might be challenging for them to behave politely and appropriately around other people. Nevertheless, there are a few things you can do to get past these obstacles and make sure they can learn and develop in social situations:

- It's crucial to explain to them in plain and simple terms what is required of them in social settings. It may entail discussing some fundamental social norms, such as how to introduce yourself and how to begin and conclude a discussion.
- Additionally, giving them regular chances to exercise these abilities in a secure setting is critical. Utilizing pictorial tools to assist them in comprehending and adhering to societal norms is another helpful strategy.
- Use image cards to help them recall important societal norms.
- Finally, it's critical to be gentle with them and show them lots of support and guidance when they succeed.

With the help of parents, educators, and tutors, they can learn how to act correctly in social situations, and teens with autism can learn to engage with others socially appropriately with the right assistance.

In Chapter 9, I will discuss how to determine if the coping skills are helping. Meet you there.

9

HOW TO DETERMINE IF THE COPING SKILLS ARE HELPING

Coping strategies for autism are effective ways to manage the effects of autism and help autistic teens to calm and relax when experiencing the effects of autism, such as tantrums, meltdowns, and anxiety.

But some parents are concerned if the coping strategies they are using for their child are working.

Below are some of the ways to determine if coping strategies are working for your child:

- Reduction in anxiety
- Reduction in tantrums and meltdowns
- Reduced sensory overload
- Increased interaction with others

- Improve communication skill

REDUCTION IN ANXIETY

Numerous autistic individuals have significant anxiety levels, although it is not a need for the autism diagnostic criteria. Despite conflicting evidence, clinical diagnoses of anxiety may be given to 40–50% of autistic persons on average.

According to the GAD diagnosis criteria, 47% of autistic persons fall into the severe anxiety group, according to a recent National Autistic Society poll.

For teenagers with autism, challenging social settings and sensory stimuli may cause more stress and anxiety.

The perception of being misunderstood and rejected by non-autistic persons contributes to anxiety. Autistic persons may disguise or camouflage to 'blend in' and not be seen as different, and it may exacerbate anxiety and harm the individual's mental health.

The following are other causes of anxiety in autistic people:

- A deviation from the norm, especially one that is unanticipated.

- The inability to recognize, comprehend, or control emotions.
- Inability to communicate needs
- Inability to interact in social settings

High anxiety levels might result in tantrums and meltdowns. Additionally, burnout and autistic fatigue may result.

The quality of an autistic teen's life, including their physical and mental health, work/school performance, and social life, may be severely impacted by this.

How to determine if coping strategies are helping your autistic teen in managing anxiety.

With coping strategies like deep breathing, mindfulness meditation, going on a nature walk, listening to relaxing music, etc., you'll notice that anxiety has less impact on them.

REDUCTION OF TANTRUMS AND MELTDOWNS

When a teen with autism experiences more stress than they can manage, meltdowns occur. When they lose control, the outcome is an eruption of anger, anxiety, tantrums, or other strong emotions.

Using coping strategies like:

- Music
- Taking a walk in a calm environment
- Exercise
- Deep inhalation
- Doing something enjoyable and unwinding.
- Using fidget and sensory toys.
- Mindfulness meditation

It will result in a decrease in tantrums and meltdowns.

Therefore, if you use or teach your autistic teen these coping strategies and you observe a decrease in meltdowns and tantrums, it is a sign that the coping strategies are working.

REDUCED SENSORY OVERLOAD

As parents of autistic teenagers, we have all seen sensory overload in teenagers with autism firsthand. It's a challenge that no child can easily overcome, and no parent likes to watch their child in pain.

When a person has sensory overload, their brain cannot absorb all the information from their five senses.

Flashing lights, loud sounds, many discussions in the same space, or someone wearing strong perfume is just a few examples of the many things that may cause sensory overload. It may be challenging for many families, particularly during the holidays when celebrations like fireworks and group get-togethers can be difficult for teenagers with autism.

But with coping strategies like:

- Taking a stroll at a nature park.
- Enjoying pleasant and relaxing music
- Relaxing via exercise
- Mindfulness
- Meditation
- Using fidget and sensory toys
- Positive visualization
- And the tranquil exercises this book offers.

Your autistic teen's sensitivity to sensory overload will lessen. That is how you can tell whether your child's coping skills are practical and work.

INCREASED INTERACTION WITH OTHERS

A recurrent topic among teens on the autism spectrum is having trouble with social contact, deciphering other people's behavior, and understanding what to say or how to behave among others.

When it comes to social interaction, teens on the autism spectrum will have a variety of preferences and habits.

Some teens on the spectrum could lack interest while engaging with others. It could only be to satisfy their basic requirements, like using their arm to grab for something that is out of their grasp. Others may have a strong desire to engage with various individuals.

Social interaction skills may be challenging for those with autism spectrum disorders, which may affect their capacity to:

- Begin or continue a discussion.
- Recognize nonverbal clues such as facial expressions and body language that provide context for what is being spoken.
- Make eye contact and keep it.
- Discuss a topic that is unrelated to their area of interest.
- Comprehend non-literal languages, such as sarcasm, idioms, and metaphors.
- Recognize when individuals use language to mask their emotions or words in a manner that obscures their intended meaning.

Some persons on the autism spectrum hyper-focus on minor details, detecting every leaf rustling in the breeze or seeing connections that others would not perceive. They are touch sensitive. Therefore they could find hand-shaking or large crowds upsetting.

Remove unimportant information, like background noise, from your system.

See how others perceive things.

Change interactions to fit social or environmental circumstances, such as altering behavior while engaging with grandparents, as opposed to classmates or coworkers.

But with coping strategies like:

- Role-play
- Self-control strategies
- Social skill development
- Social stories
- Video-modeling
- Modeling
- Relaxing via exercise
- Visualized aids

The quality of autistic teens' interactions with others will improve. It is how you determine that coping strategies are working for your child.

IMPROVE COMMUNICATION SKILLS

One of the critical signs of autism spectrum syndrome is a lack of communication skills. People with autism find it difficult to communicate their needs and desires effectively; teens with autism are no exception.

So coping strategies like:

- Role-play
- Modeling
- Video modeling
- Social stories
- Using visual aids
- Social skills development

It can help autistic teens to improve their communication skills. So, when you see an improvement in your child's communication skills, it proves that your coping strategies are working.

Bottom line

Every autistic person is unique in their strengths and interest. What works for one might not work for another person. The best strategy would be to try the coping strategies and stick with the one that best suits your child's needs.

In Chapter 10, we will explore autism spectrum disorder therapy. Happy reading.

EXPLORE AUTISM SPECTRUM DISORDER THERAPY

There are various kinds of autism therapy accessible to help individuals with Autism Spectrum Disorder. (ASD).

Autism is a continuum disease with various symptoms, including difficulties with speaking and nonverbal communication, inappropriate behaviors, repetitious behaviors, and social skills.

Early intervention for people with cognitive disabilities, such as infants and neonates, who have autism is most successful.

Early indications of autism may include a lack of laughter, social interaction, odd play abilities, aversive behaviors, and a failure to react to their name. After receiving an autistic diagnosis, various approaches, including therapies, may be beneficial.

Current treatments for autism spectrum disorders seek to reduce symptoms that interfere with everyday life and quality of life.

Teens with ASD have a variety of skills, constraints, and care requirements because ASD has an individualized impact on each person. Because of this, treatment strategies are frequently interdisciplinary and child-specific.

THE SIGNIFICANCE OF OFFERING THERAPY

Numerous therapy options are available to help teens with autism, and depending on the child's age, demeanor, requirements, and level of aptitude, a different type of treatment may be advised.

Numerous physical and emotional health problems can coexist with autism. Collaboration between therapies and practitioners can be helpful in many of these circumstances.

1. Applied Behavior Analysis (ABA)

The most popular therapy for autistic people, ABA, uses positive feedback, incentives, and penalties to help them with their social skills, verbal proficiency, and good conduct.

The following are a few of the most typical ABA goals:

- Improved communication.
- Increased verbal and passive dialogue
- Improved self-care and cleanliness
- Fostering teamwork while engaging with others.
- Decrease in maladaptive conduct.

ABA therapy is the most comprehensive program for autistics. To handle issues like effective communication, skills with coping, cognitive abilities, self-regulation, leisure and relationship skills, behavioral management, and safety skills, ABA therapy is crucial for teens with autism.

2. Relationship Development Intervention (RDI)

This approach teaches autistics how to develop relationships with their parents and other family members. This family-based treatment includes elements of fluid thinking, social interaction, and psychology.

Additionally, they will learn how to handle changes, which can be incredibly challenging. As part of the RDI program, parents receive training and act as their child's caregivers.

3. Play Therapy

Play therapy for autism is different from play therapy for other conditions. Compared to anxiety, stress, and other mental health problems, therapists are much more prescribe this form of treatment for autism.

Teens with autism gain social skills by acting, which they can relate to, thanks to playing therapy.

Autism impacts how they connect; for instance, a person with autism might focus mainly on one feature of an object and rarely participate in imaginary play. So they can interact with others through their educator by broadening their strategy and concentration.

This therapy can help them expand their play beyond their limited experiences and into interactions and group activities. With play therapy, they can investigate their environment, emotions, and relationships by pursuing their hobbies and interest.

4. Equestrian Therapy

It is frequently referred to as remedial bicycling. Teens with autism can ride horses in a secure, non-threatening setting thanks to equestrian therapy.

Both they and the animal are under the care of the trainer. Therapeutic equestrian riding, according to a study, enhances social and communication abilities while lowering restlessness and excitability.

5. *Speech therapy*

Speech therapy may be helpful for people with autism, but it isn't always the best approach because people with extreme autism may be unable to engage.

Speech therapy may be most beneficial to higher-functioning people and may help teens with ASD overcome social seclusion. A person with autism may occasionally have a concurrent condition that necessitates speech therapy.

In these situations, it may be advantageous to use a treatment approach that addresses autism and the underlying medical problem. These therapies can be given by clinicians who specialize in speech and language or by other experts.

6. *Cognitive Behavioral Therapy (CBT).*

CBT is a popular form of talk therapy where a mental health professional works with patients in a limited number of appointments that, based on the person, can last over 8 to 12 weeks.

Therapists continually improve the method to make it more reliably successful in treating nervousness and other problems.

7. Music Therapy

People with autism may find it easier to relate to their own and other people's feelings when they listen to music.

Working with a clinician while listening to music to improve social and communication skills is known as music therapy.

8. Sensory Integration

Autism can impact how sensory information is received, which could lead to sensory under or over-stimulation.

Actions that are challenging to describe can be a result of sensory information. Sensory integration can help people with ASD better handle sensory overload by allowing them to regulate sensory information.

THE SIGNIFICANCE OF GIVING THERAPY TO AUTISTIC TEENS

According to research, autism affects one in every 44 children. This high number has aided in increasing autistic recognition and growing treatment programs for the condition.

Therapies for autism have many benefits, and these benefits may last a lifetime. Recent research in the journal JAMA Pediatrics found that beginning therapy within the first year is highly beneficial for kids with early symptoms of autism. It is due to the rapid cerebral development that occurs during this period.

According to a study, twelve-month-old children who receive treatment and care have fewer social speech or repetitive behavior symptoms than elder children who did not receive therapy.

THERAPIES FOR AUTISM.

Some families discover that family therapy can help them overcome obstacles and may even help them deal with emerging problems. Consequently, they might also learn more about ASD and methods for helping their child. Couple therapy can help parents of autistic children enhance their relationship and persistence, which will help them foster stronger family bonds.

The benefit of group counseling is the chance to connect parents with others who have gone through equal things.

One survey found that after taking part, parents of children with ASD felt less anxious and more confident.

Regardless of the kind of therapy, experts suggest that kids start it as soon as they receive a diagnostic because early help improves results.

Cartooning strategies.

Using visual images in cartooning or comic strip techniques can aid in understanding the social circumstances of autistic teens. They can visualize vague or perplexing events through the creation of drawings with the assistance of an adult.

For instance, following a schoolyard altercation, your child is taken to the principal's office. They could depict the scene as an animation with speaking boxes with the assistance of an adult.

Then, an adult could discuss what transpired with your child and assist them in comprehending the emotions and thoughts of the other parties concerned.

Modeling

A model demonstrates how to act or do something, and your child follows them. They can acquire a variety of skills through modeling, including social skills like laughing and saying welcome, self-care and grooming skills, and academic duties.

Video-modeling.

Videos showcasing modeling abilities are available, but you can also create your own.

You could, for instance, film yourself, your teen, or another person participating in talks, ask a friend to participate, utilize body language, use various vocal tones, etc.

Peer Training

Peer training teaches children who struggle with social skills how to engage with and communicate with others, especially their peers and age mates.

Your autistic teen has more and better chances to develop social skills when they interact or play with others children their age. For instance, peer training might help them to understand how valuable it is for people to have a variety of talents and passions.

Additionally, they might learn how to initiate and sustain relationships with other people who have autism.

Self-control strategies

Children with autism can gain freedom by figuring out how to control their behavior.

One method is tallying papers, stamps, or a wrist clock to track a specific behavior's frequency. For instance, their goal might be to consume their meal while seated. So they can place a stamp in a journal each time they accomplish this goal.

Social-skills training

Autistic teens who receive social skills training can better understand nonverbal signals like facial expression, body language, and tone of speech.

It frequently includes abilities like putting yourself in another person's shoes, resolving interpersonal conflicts, and comprehending social and emotional norms.

They may be able to participate in a group or one-on-one social skills training program with a counselor or instructor. A few training programs offer field trips for them to practice new abilities in the neighborhood.

They can use the skills acquired in one environment to adapt to other settings, individuals, and circumstances. A counselor or instructor may create a social skills training curriculum for one or group of children.

Others might be managed by a person skilled in using specific software. These include the Stop Think Do or

PEERS (Program for the Education and Enrichment of Relational Skills) Program.

Triple P Stepping Stones

A parenting course for parents of children with developmental disabilities up to 12 is called Triple P stepping stones.

It can assist you in the following:

- Control your child's problematic behavior and growth problems.
- Encourage novel conduct.
- Establish a strong bond with your autistic child.
- Give them new talents to learn.

Behavioral therapy.

A popular ASD treatment is behavior therapy, which promotes preferred behaviors while reducing undesirable behaviors.

The majority of behavior treatments employ methods outlined by applied behavior analysis. (ABA). ABA seeks to assist a person with ASD in comprehending the relationship between actions and results.

Positive reinforcement is given to efforts at the desired behavior in ABA-based therapy. For instance, a counselor might commend a child for asking for assistance respectfully.

They are more likely to replicate the behavior because an incentive accompanies it. On the other hand, no incentive is provided if they lash out in anger or behave badly.

ABA is a method founded on research. Additionally, it is very flexible, allowing it to accommodate every child's requirements. According to studies, long-term, rigorous treatment can enhance a child's social, academic, and living skills.

Pivotal Response Therapy (PRT)

Another play-based method that adheres to ABA standards is PRT. PRT concentrates on more broad areas, such as drive, self-management, reaction to multiple signals, and the start of social encounters instead of honing in on particular behaviors.

PRT assists autistic teens in making significant advancements in their speech and social interaction skills by concentrating on these crucial areas.

A therapist may place their preferred meal or object in plain sight but out of reach during a session. This circumstance pushes them to speak up and request the object.

Since the 1970s, PRT has been researched and applied in both one-on-one and group settings. According to studies, it can help autistic teens develop their communication and interaction skills.

Discrete Trial Training (DTT)

PRT needs to be more organized than DTT, an ABA-based strategy.

Talent is divided into lesser components. A DTT strategy may involve breaking the writing process down letter by letter when training a person with ASD to write their name. Additionally, creating each character can be divided into individual strokes.

The youngster receives encouragement as they move forward through each stage.

DTT has been used successfully since the 1970s to teach skills to people with ASD.

Compared to ESDM or PRT, this exercise only entails a little free activity.

Occupational therapy and physical therapy

Some people with ASD have trouble regulating their body movements. For instance, they might walk differently than expected or struggle to write by hand.

Your child's movement abilities can develop with physical training. A child's social life and well-being can be enhanced by emphasizing stance, rhythm, equilibrium, and muscular control.

Children on the autistic spectrum can develop practical daily abilities like eating, cleaning, and clothing through occupational therapy, and occupational treatment, like physical therapy, can improve cognitive abilities.

They will learn to use help gadgets to deal with circumstances and finish chores since sessions are tailored to each person's requirements.

Two examples of such devices are speech-to-text software for a child who has trouble writing by hand and a dry-erase board for a child who has trouble communicating verbally.

Occupational Therapy

The use of everyday items and tasks of daily living, such as learning to fasten a blouse or handle a utensil correctly, are assisted by occupational therapy. However, it may entail anything related to a job, recreation, or education. The child's requirements and objectives will determine the emphasis.

What is the role of an occupational therapist?

Occupational therapist aid in establishing a particular set of goals for the autistic individual, and the goals frequently center on conduct, social contact, and academic achievement.

Evaluation and treatment are the two primary methods occupational therapists can use to develop a goal. The therapist observes to see if they are capable of performing actions that are appropriate for their age, like dressing themselves or playing a game.

They may occasionally film the child throughout the day to observe how they engage with others and their environment. It aids the therapist in figuring out what kind of treatment they require.

The therapist may pay attention to the following:

- Endurance and range of engagement.
- Change to different pursuits.
- Play skills
- The need for privacy.
- A person's reactions to contact or other types of stimulation.
- Motor abilities such as balance, stance, or handling of small items.
- Violence or other undesirable habits

- The child's interactions with the caretakers

The therapist can create a curriculum for your child after gathering information. There isn't just one therapy plan that works best. But research has shown that early, organized, personalized treatment is most effective.

Occupational therapy may incorporate many concepts, such as:

- Performing puzzles or hanging beads are examples of physical tasks that can aid in a child's balance and body awareness development.
- Playtime games that promote dialogue and engagement.
- Tasks that promote development, such as cleaning hair and teeth.
- Adaptive methods, such as passing through changes.

What are the advantages of occupational therapy for those with ASD?

Helping individuals with autism better their quality of life at home and school is the main aim of occupational therapy. So that individuals with autism can be as independent as possible, the therapy helps present, maintain, and develop everyday living skills.

Occupational therapy may be beneficial for:

- Developing daily living skills like clothing, cleaning teeth, using the bathroom, and other hygiene techniques.
- Developing Fine motor skills necessary for gripping objects in their hands while writing or using tools
- Developing motor abilities for strolling, ascending steps, or operating a horse, sitting, and good balance.
- Cognitive skills for distinguishing between different hues, forms, and sizes.
- Understanding of one's physique and how it relates to others.
- Developing Visual reading and writing Skills.
- Develop self-care, social, dialogue, problem-solving, and play skills.

With occupational therapy, a person with autism may be able to build on these abilities to:

- Build healthy relationships with other people.
- Learn to concentrate on an activity.
- Become adept at postponing pleasure.

- Use more suitable methods to express emotions.
- Play with other young people.
- Learn to control themself.

Nutritional Therapy

Some autistic children experience stomach problems as well as problems with their bones. Additionally, some might express a dislike for particular tastes or textures, such as the soft, squishy texture of vegetables or the irregular texture of cereal.

So, while satisfying their dietary requirements is essential, doing so can be challenging. Nutritional therapy can help them maintain a nutritious diet if they are fussy about food.

You and your autistic teen can collaborate with a nutritional expert to develop a food plan that takes into account their requirements and tastes. You can also make changes to your child's dietary practices at home.

Consider the meals they enjoy, and offer them foods with comparable flavors or sensations. For more variation, if they enjoy French fries, for instance, give them a portion of sweet potato fries.

Serve both fresh meals and new exciting flavors. It lets you retain some comfort while also adding new components. Keep the amounts modest until they genuinely express a preference for the new meal.

Allowing them to choose from various novel dietary choices will give them a feeling of control. Green beans, broccoli, and asparagus could be on the menu.

Integrated Play Groups

Teens with and without autistic spectrum disorders are mixed in IPGs so those with ASD can imitate their classmates and pick up playing skills.

Each group consists of three to five people, only a few of whom have ASD.

If your child participates in IPGs, they may begin to role-play more frequently over time. They will have many opportunities to develop social skills while interacting with others.

IPGs can gather once a week for up to three hours. According to research, children with ASD who participated in two 30-minute IPG lessons per week for four months demonstrated improvements in the content of their play, how they used their objects, and how well they interacted with their classmates.

Floortime

Play therapy and floortime are very similar, but the foundation of floortime is that parents should strive to widen their autistic child's "circles of communication." To put it another way, parents can urge their children to engage in back-and-forth communication (verbal or nonverbal), which can be extremely difficult for those with autism spectrum disorders.

Floortime helps autistic children in developing their social skills and form mental bonds.

Parents should participate in their child's games during floortime, and the child should follow their example, and parents, caretakers, and even elder relatives can lead sessions.

Floortime can be performed anywhere and last for about 20 minutes or longer.

Through internet classes, movies, literature, or engaging with a Floortime practitioner, parents can learn about Floortime and its methods.

Parent-Child Interaction Therapy (PCIT)

PCIT for Aggressive Behaviors is a form of parent-child interaction therapy.

A sizeable percentage of teens with autistic spectrum disorders exhibit violent behaviors, making it extremely challenging to exit the house or participate in everyday activities.

Parents who have received expert training administer the Parent-Child Interaction Therapy (PCIT) method to children who exhibit violent tendencies.

With PCIT, "Parents learn to integrate explicit limit-setting within the framework of a dominant relationship to stop a pattern of increasing unfavorable behaviors between parent and child".

According to PCIT, effective limit-setting and consistent punishment depend on a robust and safe bonding connection. It improves both adults' and kids' mental health.

TREATMENTS FOR THE CONDITIONS THAT FREQUENTLY GO ALONG WITH AUTISM.

Autism frequently coexists with certain physical disorders. Here are a few instances of typical ailments and potential remedies.

Aggression.

Some autistic teens express their anguish by acting aggressively, like striking or screaming. It would help if you first comprehend what they are attempting to communicate to you to handle this situation.

Certain circumstances or triggers, like sounds, make them uncomfortable.

Cognitive behavioral therapy (CBT) can assist them in finding healthier methods to communicate their needs.

Anxiety.

High-stress levels or conditions like OCD and obsessive-compulsive disorder can be challenging for teens with ASD Anxiety can lead to destructive actions like tantrums or trouble interacting with others.

There are numerous approaches to managing anxiety. One useful tactic might be to help them to recognize their nervous emotions. It is also beneficial to gradually expose them to the cause of their anxiety in a secure setting.

Sleep problems.

Teens with ASD may struggle to get enough sleep at night due to restlessness and other sleep disruptions, and concentration and temperament can be negatively impacted by sleep deprivation.

Therefore, practicing excellent sleep habits, such as creating a relaxing ritual before bed, is crucial.

ADHD) (Attention Deficit Disorder)

Impulsive behavior or inattentiveness may be symptoms of ADHD in individuals with ASD, which can impair academic or social functioning.

Concentration can be enhanced by promoting restful sleep and regular exercise.

GI (gastrointestinal) problems.

GI complaints, such as stomach discomfort, swelling, and diarrhea, are frequently experienced by children with ASD. According to some studies, GI issues may contribute to these other problems, including irritability and sleep disruptions.

You can help them solve GI issues by reducing tension, promoting exercise, increasing fiber and water consumption, and monitoring which meals make them uncomfortable.

MAXIMIZING THE BENEFITS OF THERAPY.

Although a trained therapist will assist your child during therapies, you still have some parental responsibility.

You can take these extra measures as you research your child's therapy choices to make sure the meetings are very productive.

Begin early

Therapy efficacy may be increased with early involvement. You don't necessarily need to wait for a confirmed diagnosis to start thinking about therapy choices or even start using some techniques at home.

Don't wait to begin therapy once a formal diagnosis and alternatives exist. The key is to start early.

Not all of the therapy options you attempt will work for your teen. You can, however, experiment with several therapies at once and watch for good signs of progress, and you will move closer to discovering what works with each therapy you try.

Speech-language therapy and dietary therapy are effective therapies that coexist without being detrimental.

Continue with the therapy at home.

Sometimes therapy will lead you and your autistic teen through exercises you can do at home. You can use play-based exercises from PRT and ESDM at home.

It is significant for many reasons:

- It allows you more time to spend with your child and get to know them better.
- Home therapies can also support the development of abilities acquired during therapy appointments.
- They may give you more parental confidence.

Create a routine.

Consider your child's safety as you research therapy choices, and when they adhere to a routine, teens with ASD frequently flourish.

Maintain a plan that includes treatment appointments whenever you can, and let them know if it might alter.

Consider their strength.

Be on the lookout for places where they shine. For instance, they might have a talent for singing or a keen eye for precision.

You can also keep them interested by applying their skills to incentives and ASD therapy at home. And always keep in mind that your child still has plenty of space to develop, despite any challenges they may be experiencing.

YOUR OPINION MATTERS

Thanks for taking your time to read this book and If you found *"Coping Skills for Teens with Autism"* to be helpful, leaving a review will be a great way to express your gratitude. By sharing your experience, you can provide valuable insights and information that can assist others in making an informed decision.

Leaving a review can help bring awareness to this community, and your positive words can provide hope and comfort to families and individuals who are going through similar experiences.

Scan the *QR code* below to leave a review

OTHER BOOKS BY
R ROBINSON

Visit **http://www.r-robinson-books.com/** or Scan the **QR code** below

CONCLUSION

There are many various kinds of coping strategies for teens with autism, and because all teens are unique, no one method will be effective. So you need to study and discover the best coping strategies for your child.

As an illustration, some people stroll while listening to music, others practice deep breathing exercises, and others go outside and take in the scenery.

The bottom line is that it's critical to assist your autistic teen in identifying the coping strategies that are most effective for them.

With the help of the coping strategies discussed in this book, you will certainly find the ones that best work for your child.

BIBLIOGRAPHY

https://www.aspriscs.co.uk/news-blogs/signs-and-symptoms-of-autism-in-teenagers/

https://raisingchildren.net.au/autism/learning-about-autism/assessment-diagnosis/signs-of-asd-in-teens

https://www.healthline.com/health/autism-in-teens

https://www.mayoclinic.org/diseases-conditions/autism-spectrum-disorder/symptoms-causes/syc-20352928

https://newfocusacademy.com/riding-the-emotional-meltdown-alongside-teens-with-autism/

https://newfocusacademy.com/emotional-meltdowns-and-autism-working-through-tantrums/

https://www.healthychildren.org/English/ages-stages/teen/Pages/Mental-Health-and-Teens-Watch-for-Danger-Signs.aspx

https://www.spectrumnews.org/news/autistic-burnout-explained/

https://childresidentialtreatment.com/autism-meltdown-triggers/

https://www.verywellhealth.com/autism-and-sensory-overload-259892

https://www.autismparentingmagazine.com/coping-skills-reducing-overwhelm/

https://www.fortbehavioral.com/addiction-recovery-blog/4-coping-skills-teens-should-know-for-mental-health/

https://www.discovercampworth.com/autism-treatment-center-fort-worth-texas-blog/coping-skills-for-teens-with-autism/

https://www.helpguide.org/articles/autism-learning-disabilities/helping-your-child-with-autism-thrive.htm

https://parents.au.reachout.com/skills-to-build/wellbeing/things-to-try-coping-skills-and-resilience/teach-your-teenager-coping-skills-for-wellbeing

https://www.newportacademy.com/resources/well-being/relaxation-skills-for-teens/

https://www.newportacademy.com/resources/empowering-teens/coping-skills-teens/
https://hiddentalentsaba.com/activities-for-autistic-teenager/
https://behaviortlc.com/blog/calming-strategies-for-asd/
https://hiddentalentsaba.com/activities-for-autistic-teenager/
https://www.autismparentingmagazine.com/creating-inner-peace-the-benefits-of-yoga-for-children-with-autism-spectrum-disorder/
https://raisingchildren.net.au/autism/school-play-work/school/anxiety-at-school-asd
https://www.autismspeaks.org/blog/back-school-17-tips-help-autistic-kids
https://www.sarahdooleycenter.org/news/autism-in-the-classroom-how-to-handle-behavior-challenges/
https://thespectrum.org.au/autism-strategy/social-interaction/
https://edukania.com/how-to-teach-autistic-children-to-behave-appropriately-in-social-gatherings/
https://www.songbirdcare.com/articles/types-of-therapy-for-autism
https://www.webmd.com/brain/autism/therapies-to-help-with-autism
https://www.helpguide.org/articles/autism-learning-disabilities/autism-treatments-therapies-interventions.htm

Printed in Great Britain
by Amazon